CAIRN TERRIER BIBLE
AND
CAIRN TERRIERS

Your Complete Cairn Terrier Guide

COVERS CAIRN TERRIERS, CAIRN TERRIER PUPPIES,
CAIRN TERRIER TRAINING, CAIRN TERRIER NUTRITION,
CAIRN TERRIER HEALTH, HISTORY, BREEDING, & MORE!

By Mark Manfield

© DYM Worldwide Publishers, 2019.

Published by DYM Worldwide Publishers 2019.

ISBN: 978-1-911355-91-5

will not be liable for, the websites being temporarily or being removed from the Internet. The accuracy and completeness of the information provided herein, and opinions stated herein are not guaranteed or warranted to produce any particular results, and the advice or strategies, contained herein may not be suitable for every individual. The author, publisher, distributors, and/or affiliates shall not be liable for any loss incurred as a consequence of the use and application, directly or indirectly of any information presented in this work. This publication is designed to provide information regarding the subject matter covered. The information included in this book has been compiled to give an overview of the topics covered. The information contained in this book has been compiled to provide an overview of the subject. It is not intended as medical advice and should not be construed as such. For a firm diagnosis of any medical conditions, you should consult a doctor or veterinarian (as related to animal health). The writer, publisher, distributors, and/or affiliates of this work are not responsible for any damages or negative consequences following any of the treatments or methods highlighted in this book.

Website links are for informational purposes only and should not be seen as a personal endorsement; the same applies to any products or services mentioned in this work. The reader should also be aware that although the web links included were correct at the time of writing they may become out of date in the future. Any pricing or currency exchange rate information was accurate at the time of writing but may become out of date in the future. The Author, Publisher, distributors, and/or affiliates assume no responsibility for pricing and currency exchange rates mentioned within this work.

Table of Contents

Cairn Terrier Navigation Guide – How to Maximize This Guide

Welcome! Whether you are thinking about purchasing a Cairn Terrier, or you already have one and want to understand more about the breed, this book will give you everything you need to know. Each chapter is packed with interesting facts and information that will expand your knowledge, improve the life of your dog, and most importantly solidify the bond between you and your Cairn.

The most important aspect of owning a Cairn Terrier is understanding that it's a partnership for the life of your dog, and for much of yours.

Chapter 1: Have you ever wondered where the Cairn Terrier originated from? In this chapter, you will find out exactly how this extraordinary dog came to be, as well as some interesting facts about your breed.

Chapter 2: Are you thinking about buying a Cairn Terrier puppy? Find out everything you need to know to make an informed and intelligent decision, in this chapter.

Chapter 3: After reading chapter two, you have now made the decision that you want to purchase a Cairn Terrier. The question is how can you find a reputable breeder? What are the tell-tale signs of a bad breeder? You will find out the answers to these questions and much more in this chapter.

Chapter 4: Maybe you have decided that you would rather buy your Cairn Terrier from a source other than a breeder, in chapter four, you will learn about the other choices that are available to you.

Chapter 5: Cairn Terriers come in a variety of colors, they are also bred with other dogs to produce some interesting mixes, you will learn all about them in this chapter.

Chapter 6: So, you have taken the plunge and decided to purchase a Cairn Terrier, congratulations! Your journey with this wonderfully vibrant dog has only just begun. Learn what you will need to do to ensure your puppy's transition into his new environment, is perfect for him.

Chapter 7: Dogs need to eat, but if this is your first time owning a Cairn, feeding decisions can become overwhelming. Learn what to feed your dog, when to feed your dog, and most importantly, what not to feed him.

Chapter 8: If you want a good relationship with your dog, you will need to train him to be obedient. In this chapter, you will learn how to teach your dog basic commands such as sit, stand, down and come. You will also learn how to house train and discipline your dog.

Chapter 9: It is important that you groom your Cairn Terrier properly, you will learn how to bath, cut his nails, clean his teeth and much more in this chapter.

Chapter 10: If you want your dog to live a long life, the right exercise is just as important as the right diet. It will also keep him from getting bored and frustrated, and ultimately from becoming a nightmare dog.

Chapter 11: In an ideal world, your Cairn Terrier would never get sick, and he would live forever! Unfortunately, we don't live in an ideal world, and there is a possibility that he could get sick. Learn all about the most common health issues that a Cairn Terrier might suffer from.

Chapter 12: Your love for Cairn Terriers has become so strong that you want them to fill the earth! Not literally, but you know what I mean! Learn everything you need to know about breeding Cairn Terriers in this chapter.

Chapter 13: Unfortunately, accidents do happen, and it is important that you are ready and prepared when they do. This chapter will teach you everything you need to handle an emergency situation.

Chapter 14: Buying a dog is not as simple as picking him up from a shelter and bringing him home. There are rules and regulations you need to follow, if not, you could face a hefty fine. Don't cut any corners and make sure you are compliant with the legal requirements for owning a Cairn Terrier in your country.

Chapter 15: Concluding thoughts and summary- If you haven't made the decision that you want to become a Cairn Terrier owner yet, now is the time to do so.

Bonus Chapter: Whether you are from the United States, Australia, Canada, or the United Kingdom, there is something in this chapter for everyone!

CHAPTER 1

Cairn Terrier Origins: How Did It All Begin?

The history of Scottish Terriers similar to the modern Cairn Terrier, a form or ancestor of which date back hundreds of years, at least to the 1500s. They were referenced in writings, as early as the time of King James I., in the early 1600s. They were originally bred to hunt small animals in the cairns (dens within the rock), in Scotland.

As the name suggests, they are from the Terrier family. The word Terrier originates from the Latin root word 'terra,' which means earth. The name is well applied since the purpose of the dog is to work underneath the ground getting rid of rodents and other animals that destroy country living.

Cairn Terriers are not only cute and adorable,
they also have a rich and interesting history.

Where Are Cairn Terriers From? Cairn Terrier History

Except for the German Miniature Schnauzer, all Terrier breeds originate from the British Isles. They fall into two basic categories, the smooth-coated, long-legged dogs of England, and the rough-coated short-legged dogs of Scotland. The Scottish bred Terriers are made up of the Skye Terrier, the Cairn Terrier, the West Highland White Terrier, and the Modern Scottish Terrier. At the beginning of the 1800's, any one of these breeds were known as Scotch Terriers. Interbreeding was the norm during this time, and any of these breeds could come from one litter without it being unusual. The color of the dog would determine how a pup was classified.

When breeders began to exhibit at dog shows, it was decided that there needed to be more uniformity within the breed. For example, all pups within a litter should be of the same type of their sire and dam, and they should resemble each other.

Most of the early history of the Cairn is focused on the Isle of Skye, if you look at Skye on a map, you will notice that it is a very remote town positioned at the west side of the Highlands. It is also connected to the Inner Hebrides, a land famous for its smooth Scotsmen and its rugged topography, where a strong and bold dog was needed to take control of vermin. The Cairn was the perfect candidate to drive out the vermin from fields, stables, and houses. They were also required to get rid of foxes and badgers.

The history of the Cairn Terrier is complex, but it is believed that Captain Mac Leod of Drynck on the Isle of Skye bred the first strain of Cairn Terrier. The Mac Donald's of Watermist bred Cairns of brindle and gray colors, and the Mac Kinnons of Kilbride bred the dark brindle, red and cream Cairns. This is how the Cairn Terriers of today began.

The Cairn was originally named the Short-Haired Skye Terrier and on the mainland, he was known as the Tod-hunter.

The Cairn Terrier has been around for a long time, it was one of the first Terrier breeds and it is also one of the most well-known thanks to the character Toto, in *The Wizard of Oz*.

Understanding Your Cairn Terrier – Some Interesting Facts

1. It was not until the early 20th century that Cairn Terriers were bred for appearance.
2. Cairn Terriers are very good therapy dogs.

3. The American Kennel Club first registered the Cairn Terrier in 1913.

4. Yes, there are some famous Cairn Terriers, but one of the things they are most famous for is digging up lawns and flowerbeds!

5. The Cairn Terrier is one of the most popular breeds of dogs and is ranked at number 69 by the American Kennel Club.

6. Cairn Terriers are possessive of their food and toys. They don't like people touching what belongs to them.

7. There are no white Cairn Terriers.

8. Cairn Terriers are very sensitive dogs, and get upset easily.

9. Cairn Terriers who have not been trained properly will bark uncontrollably, until they get what they want!

10. Cairn Terriers might growl and act aggressively, if they are not getting enough attention.

11. The Cairn Terrier is one of the most ancient Terriers.

12. Several famous people own or have owned a Cairn Terrier including Shelley Duvall, George Kennedy, David Hasselhoff, Bill Murray, J. Edgar Hoover, and Liza Minnelli.

13. Cairn Terriers have appeared in the TV series *George Lopez*, and *I Love Lucy*.

14. The Cairn Terrier who played Toto in *The Wizard of Oz*, and also starred in the Shirley Temple movie *Bright Eyes*, as well as many other movies.

Famous Cairn Terriers - Was Toto A Cairn Terrier?

"And Toto, too?" is one of the most iconic statements ever spoken in a movie! Yes, Toto was a brindle Cairn Terrier; his real name was Terry, and he starred in the Movie *The Wizard of Oz,* in 1939.

Cairn Terriers are extremely intelligent dogs,
they always make good characters in films!

Cairn Terrier Height - How Tall Will He Grow?

The Cairn Terrier is a small dog and will stop growing at approximately 9 (22.9 cm) to 10 inches (25.4cm).

Cairn Terrier Size and Cairn Terrier Weight – How Much Do Cairn Terriers Weigh? How Will I know When My Cairn Terrier Is Full Grown?

The Cairn Terrier weighs between 13 (5.89kg) to 14 pounds (6.35kg). Most small dogs are fully grown, by the time they are one year old.

Cairn Terrier Temperament – What Should I Expect From My Cairn Terrier Personality?

The Cairn Terrier is a tiny little dog with a larger than life personality. Despite their size, they are bold and fearless dogs. If you are looking for a dog to sit with and stroke all day, this is not the dog for you because they are very energetic and hyperactive, they like to keep busy, and are always ready to get their paws dirty! They require a lot of activity and stimulation, if not, they will get bored, start acting up, and become very destructive.

They treat small animals such as mice, cats and rabbits as prey, to avoid this problem, early socialization with other animals, is required.

The Cairn is a predictable dog, there are no surprises with him; although he is bred for the outdoors, he fits in well with family life. He loves children, and gets along well with strangers, once he learns to trust them. He is a feisty dog, you won't catch him looking for trouble, but if it comes to him, he will stand his ground as if he were 10 feet tall.

Due to their hunting background, Cairn Terriers have a strong desire to work; their teeth are strong, powerful, and large, in comparison to their bodies. They have very good eyesight and hearing. Although they have been bred for generations, the purpose for their existence remains the same.

If you like working with your dog, you will find that the Cairn is always happy and willing to do so, he is intelligent and enjoys a challenge, he also likes to please his owner. Give him a job where his brain power is required, and he is in his element. However, due to his intelligent nature, he will attempt to push your buttons, which is why it is important to let him know who is boss, the moment you get him as a pet.

If you are a first-time dog owner, it is essential that you take your responsibilities seriously, because if he sees something he likes, he can run off at any time. You will always need to keep your Cairn Terrier on a leash. If your garden has a fence, you will need to secure the bottom of it with concrete, and make sure that it is high enough, also. Cairn Terriers don't like being restricted, and will either dig underneath the fence, or, if it is low enough, climb over it to get out. Never leave your Cairn Terrier outside without keeping an eye on him, or he will attempt to escape. When you take him out for a walk, and he is not on a leash, he will run across a busy street with no regard for traffic, if he sees a squirrel or any other animal that he considers prey. They also tend to chase garbage blowing in the wind. Therefore, you will always need to keep him on a leash.

When it comes to obedience, Cairns have a rebellious streak. As stated, they are intelligent dogs, but they are also very independent, and together, these characteristics make for a very sassy dog. Don't let their height fool you, training a Cairn Terrier is hard work. He is an alert and fast dog, and wants to be equal to his owner.

Cairn Terrier Pictures – What Do Cairn Terriers Look Like?

Cairn Terriers are cute and adorable dogs, they come in many different shaggy colored coats, making them look slightly scruffy. They are small dogs with wide heads and tiny erect pointed ears. They have short tails, to match their short bodies.

Purebred Cairn Terriers come in a wide range of colors.

Cairn Terriers are known for their sassyness, but they make great companions!

Cairn Terriers love to keep busy; they are very active dogs.

CHAPTER 2

What Do I Need To Know Before Buying A Cairn Terrier?

S o you are thinking about buying a Cairn Terrier? That's great, but before you go out and purchase one, there are a few things you need to know about this wonderful dog.

Owning Cairn Terriers – What Do I Need To Know?

A Cairn Terrier Is For Life

The most important thing to understand about owning a dog, whether it's a Cairn Terrier or any other breed, is that dogs are for life! The Cairn lives to approximately 17 years of age, on average, so he will be with you for a good few years! If you are not prepared to make the commitment required for a dog to live a good life, then don't get one. The highest number of internet searches for dogs take place during the holiday season, and many people start buying puppies in the first few weeks of November. Sadly, within a month, once the reality of owning a dog sets in, many are abandoned. Most dogs are abandoned between 23rd and 27th of December.

Cairn Terrier puppies are hard work,
do you have what it takes to raise one?

Cairn Terriers Love To Play

If you are looking for a dog who will sit at home all day and watch your favorite TV shows with you, then the Cairn Terrier is not for you. They are extremely hyperactive dogs- and love to play and play and play!

Cairn Terriers Are Time Consuming

Your life is not going to be the same once you bring a dog into the home. You are going to have to sacrifice your time and take responsibility for the new addition to your family. Puppies are like babies, their needs come before your own. Get up and go will no longer be your mantra, as you will have to think about your dog before you make any decision. If you want to go on vacation, unless you are staying in a pet-friendly hotel, you will need to arrange a babysitter for your Cairn. This is another cost you will need to factor into your budget.

Cairn Terriers Cost Money

There is no such thing as a cheap dog, so if you don't have the cash to spare, don't buy one! Your Cairn will need plenty of food and water, bedding, toys, collars, leashes, and a host of other accessories to make him happy. You will also need to make regular trips to the vet.

Cairn Terriers Need Exercise

Because of the intelligent nature of the Cairn Terrier, they need mental as well as physical stimulation. Not only will you have to take him for walks every day, you will also need to make sure he is mentally stimulated, or he will get bored and start acting up.

Cairn Terriers Change Color

If you don't want to end up with a black dog, don't buy a red or gray brindle Cairn, because by the time they are four years old, they are almost pure black.

Cairn Terrier Cost - How Much Does It Cost To Look After a Cairn Terrier?

As stated, if you can't afford to make the financial commitment required to get a dog, then don't buy one! Cairn Terriers are not cheap, once you have made your initial purchase there are going to be ongoing costs. Including food, vet and insurance bills you are looking at spending an estimated $1600 a year (£1202 at the time of this writing), which amounts to $19,200 (£14,428) over a lifetime.

Cairn Terrier Toy - What Type Of Toys Do Cairn Terriers Prefer?

Cairn Terriers love to play, and there are plenty of toys you can purchase to help satisfy their high energy levels.

- **Treat Ball:** This toy will make your dog work for their food or treat. It is a sturdy ball made from durable plastic. There is a small compartment that releases food and treats when the ball is pushed around. There is a clear piece of plastic over the top, so you can see when it needs refilling. You can also twist it open, for easy cleaning.
- **Flying Squirrel:** Made from a long-lasting heavy canvas material, this toy fly's a fair distance when thrown so that your dog can chase it. The paws glow in the dark, making it easy to find, and it also floats in water.
- **Chew Textured Toy:** If your Cairn is an aggressive chewer, this toy is perfect for him. Made from a nylon material, it has been designed for your dog to chew on it for hours. The bone is textured, so while your dog is chewing, it is also cleaning his teeth, removing the tartar and plaque buildup.

Cairn Terrier Adaptability - How Well Do Cairn Terriers Adapt To a New Environment?

Moving into a new environment can be stressful for a Cairn Terrier. Similar to the way it would be if we as humans move to a place we are not familiar with, surrounded by strangers who don't speak the same language as us, don't look like us or don't share the same cultural habits. It would take a while for us to adjust, the same is true for dogs. When your Cairn enters his new environment, there are people, sounds, sights, and rules that he will need to get used to, before he feels completely comfortable.

Some Cairns might settle right into their new home and feel totally relaxed as soon as they arrive. However, this is generally not the case for adopted Terriers, they go through a transition period which can last for one to two days, or a few months.

The dog will spend this time testing the environment, and answering the question "what is expected here?" What am I allowed to do, and what am I not allowed to do? How are these people different than the other people I have been around? What are the safe and danger zones? This transition period is going to take patience on your part, so don't get discouraged if you feel your new dog is not adapting fast enough.

Some dogs become quite fearful in a new environment, and it will take longer for them to adapt. Even though Cairn Terriers are naturally bold dogs, there might be an initial period of shyness while he is getting used to you. This behavior is often displayed through growling, trembling, hiding, barking, or avoiding contact. He might show signs of self-mutilation through chewing or licking himself, pacing, whining, submissive urination, and anorexia.

Giving fearful dogs control over the rate at which they interact or engage with new people, animals or anything else in their new environment will help them to become more confident. Don't try and force your dog to get over his fear by putting him in situations he is not comfortable with, such treatment will make him even more nervous, and he may possibly start to even look at you with suspicion. Reward your dog with high-value treats when he does well in new social situations, this will give him the incentive to let his guard down and start trusting the people around him.

If your dog is so fearful that he starts to bite people, you will need to contact a behavior specialist immediately. This behavior is not going to go away or get better on its own, the longer he is left to continue acting like this, the worse he will get.

Adolescent Cairns, whether they have been adopted or raised in a home tend to display a lot of demand behavior, barking, jumping, nipping, pulling on the leash etc. This behavior is natural for the stage of life he is in, and many of the behaviors might have been acceptable to the previous owner, so he is simply used to acting like this. Practice careful management, supervision, and training of desirable replacement behaviors, to help your new dog adapt to the rules of his new environment.

Miniature Cairn Terriers -Do They Exist? What Do I Need To Know?

Miniature dogs are ideal for individuals and families who don't have much space to spare, or who won't be too much of a threat to their children. According to the American Kennel Club (AKC) there are no standard weight or height requirements for a dog to be considered miniature. These limitations are set by the breeds individual national breed club. However, there are certain characteristics that place some dogs into the miniature category.

Miniature Dog Breed Characteristics

When using the term "miniature" dog, there are two distinct meanings:

1. Miniature can refer to a dog that is smaller than the larger average for their particular breed. For example, the miniature Doberman.
2. Miniature can mean that some dogs are just naturally smaller than others.

Why Choose a Miniature Dog?

There are a variety of reasons as to why someone will want to purchase a miniature dog, here are some of them:

They are cute: Miniature dogs are perhaps the most adorable little creatures you will ever lay eyes on. They don't grow, and stay that size for the duration of their lives, so it's basically like having a puppy for life.

Families With Small Children: Although it is a well-known fact that dogs like children. Large dogs can be quite intimidating, and parents might worry that they might knock down or hurt their young kids.

Families Living In Small Accommodation: Large dogs can take up a lot of space, and if a family lives in a two-bedroom apartment with no backyard, it will be too difficult to cater to the needs of a larger dog.

People That Can't Cope With Large Dogs: There are people who might want a large dog but are not able to handle one because of physical impairment. While all dogs are capable of being trained to behave well, when they reach their golden years, there are going to be times when they need help from their owners. This is especially true when it comes to grooming, getting in and out of a vehicle, and going up and down stairs. Dogs need to be able to rely on their owner, and someone who is physically impaired will find it difficult to cope with the demands of a large dog.

Miniature Vs. Small Dogs: By definition, Cairn Terriers are not miniature dogs, but small dogs. There is no larger version of the Cairn Terrier, and neither are they considered miniature in comparison to other miniature dogs. However, small and miniature dogs do share similar characteristics.

Napoleon Complex: We have all heard of the term "Napoleon Complex" in humans – when a person of a short stature feels as if they must make up for their lack of height, with domineering and overly-aggressive social behavior. Well, small and miniature dogs suffer from the Napoleon Complex! For one, they get away with behaviors that would not be tolerated from larger dogs. Biting, snarling, running away when called, and pulling on the leash are generally viewed as a defense mechanism protecting their short stature. But if they are not corrected early, such behaviors can quickly turn into a habit. Owners should keep in mind that regardless of the size of the dog, such behavior is unacceptable, the good news is that with the right training and socialization, this won't be a problem for very long.

Feeding Requirements: Small breeds have different calorie intake needs than large dogs. Small dogs have a bigger surface area per lb / kg than large dogs, meaning that they consume energy at a faster rate for doing normal things, such as keeping warm and walking.

Cairn Terrier Puppies - What Do I Need To Know?

Cairn Terrier puppies are adorable! They are loved by their owners and everyone else around them. They are affectionate and cute little beings that you don't want to let out of your sight. Here are a few things you will need to know about your Cairn Terrier puppy.

Feeding: Young puppies need feeding three to four times per day. Their bowel and bladder muscles are not fully developed, so you will need to take them outside to use the bathroom as soon as they have finished eating or drinking. This helps with the house-training process. Prepare for accidents, get ready to do a lot of cleaning up and don't get mad at your dog when it does happen, because they have not been fully house trained.

You Will Lose Some Sleep: Just like a newborn baby, your Cairn will wake you up several times a night. It might be because he needs to go to the toilet, or because he is bored and wants something to do.

You should not leave your puppy alone for more than a few hours; when he is alone, it's best for him to stay in a crate. This helps with the house-training process, and will keep your house in one piece! Puppies tend to chew things up, especially your most loved and expensive items. You will also need to bear in mind that puppies can't hold their bladders and bowels, for more than a few hours.

They Have No Manners: Put bluntly, Cairn puppies are destructive, they enjoy going on excursions around the house and will lick, chew, and even eat things in their new environment. They have yet to grasp an understanding of what it means to have manners, and they are very hyperactive and unruly. Cairn Terriers need extensive training and socialization, it will take a while before your puppy learns how to behave himself around people.

Are you prepared to come home from work and spend your lunch breaks caring for your puppy? Will you be able to cope with being woken up several times throughout the night? Do you have the time to dedicate several hours a week to socialization and training? Do you have other pets or children in your home that will find it difficult to cope with a puppy? These are all questions you will need to ask yourself before buying a Cairn Terrier puppy.

If you feel as if a puppy is too much for you to handle at this stage, and you don't have the extra time to spare, you might want to consider adopting an adult dog instead.

Cairn Terrier Agility - Is The Cairn Terrier Fast?

If you are looking for a running partner, you are not going to get very far with a Cairn Terrier. They do love to run, and they will take off in a quick gallop if you let them off the lead. However, speed is not one of their strong points.

The speed that a dog can run depends on the breed and its body composition. Short-legged breeds such as Cairn Terriers and Dachshunds are nowhere near as fast as long-legged runners, like Whippets and Greyhounds.

All dogs share similar qualities in terms of the way they were designed for running:

- **Feet:** Dogs feet have got incredible gripping power, they are able to feel the ground beneath them, in addition, they have nails for traction, which gives them powerful turning ability and complex gaits.

- **Power and forward drive:** Because of their long loins, flexible spine and strong abdominal muscles, dogs have got plenty of power and forward drive.

When dogs run fast, it looks like they are galloping like horses, they possess a four-time asymmetrical gait, which means that when they are running, their feet fall in a certain pattern. One foot will lift off the ground, before the other corresponding foot behind it steps down. Some of the faster breeds have a double suspension gallop in which their body is catapulted into the air with all four legs leaving the ground simultaneously.

The average speed for a dog is between 10 and 20 miles per hour; some dogs are much faster, and others much slower than this.

Cairn Terrier Playfulness – Are Cairn Terriers Playful Dogs?

Cairn Terrier dogs are very playful; they will play with you and they will play with other dogs that cross their path. Playing means something entirely different to dogs than it does to humans, and sometimes, owners can misinterpret when dogs are interacting with each other whether it's mistaking innocent play for fighting, or actual aggressive behavior for playing. Therefore, it's important to understand the language your Cairn is speaking, when he is playing.

Dog to dog play is a series of repetitive and active behaviors that have different meanings depending on the context. Playing helps dogs develop physically and emotionally because it relies on their ability to read verbal and non-verbal communication. Dogs that are forbidden from playing, or are not given the opportunity to play, end up deficient in several important developmental areas.

Understanding Dog Play

- If your Cairn is too rough when playing, he should not be allowed to play with other dogs until he learns to play without being aggressive.
- Teaching your dog to back off, before play gets too aggressive, will give him some time to calm down before allowing him to go back to the group.
- Fights are avoided when both dogs understand the rules of the game; that is when they both allow each other to win. The more excited dogs become, the more likely it is that a mock battle becomes a real one.
- A mature dog is confident in his abilities and will look for other dogs to play with. They are capable of giving the right signals so that other dogs do not become too overwhelmed or excited.

Most dogs enjoy safe playtime together by relying on a series of signals that communicate their playfulness. These signals include licking, itching, yawning, sneezing, and sniffing. If the signals are recognized by the dogs, it is safe to continue playing, if not, things are about to get heated, and human intervention is required.

Cairn Terrier Barking - Do Cairn Terriers Bark Often?

Expecting a dog not to bark is like expecting a child not to talk. Barking is a form of vocal communication, and what your dog means when he barks will depend on the situation. In general, dogs bark for the following reasons:

Alarm/Fear: If a noise or object startles a dog and catches their attention, they will bark. This can happen at any time and in any location.

Territorial/Protective: When an animal or another person enters an area, your dog believes is his territory, he will bark. This type of barking is often excessive because he feels as if he is being threatened. As the perceived threat gets closer, the barking will get louder, and he will appear alert and aggressive.

Attention Seeking: Some dogs bark because they want something, they might want a treat, they might want to go outside, or it could be just to get their owner's attention.

Greeting/Play: Dogs get excited when they greet people or other animals. It's a happy bark accompanied by jumping and tail wagging.

Separation Anxiety: When left alone, dogs with separation anxiety bark excessively. They may also display other symptoms such as inappropriate elimination, depression, destructiveness, and pacing.

Compulsive Barking: Compulsive barkers bark for the sake of it, it is possible that they enjoy the sound of their own voice. They will also do things excessively, such as run along a fence, or run around in circles, continuously.

However, Cairn Terriers are known to bark a lot; because they are born and bred to hunt, an important part of their communication system is to bark. They have got a strong prey drive, and they are always ready for action. When they are hunting underground, Terriers use a high-pitched bark to sound the alarm, and let the hunting party know where they are.

Cairn Terriers are also very alert dogs, you could say they are nosey and want to get involved in whatever is going on around them. They are very curious, and it is a part of their DNA to bark. Pay attention to their barking as soon as you hear it.

Once they are satisfied that you have noticed them, they will stop. Instinctive behavior is difficult to control, so if their barking is causing too much disturbance in your household, you might want to contact an animal behaviorist to help. Don't punish your Terrier for barking as this will confuse him, as far as he is concerned, he is only doing what comes natural to him.

When Do Cairn Terriers Calm Down?

Cairn Terriers are very hyperactive dogs naturally, they don't start calming down on their own, until they begin reaching their golden years.

Cairn Terriers and Separation Anxiety – Do Cairn Terriers Suffer From Separation Anxiety?

Separation anxiety is normal in Cairn Terrier puppies. It typically happens when they realize they have been isolated from the pack. Puppies are born into litters, and they spend their first few weeks with their siblings until they are moved to different homes. When they realize this, they will howl, cry, and bark when left alone. Within a week, they will learn that even though you leave them alone, you will come back eventually. You can help your puppy overcome separation anxiety quicker by leaving a ticking clock, a hot water bottle, stuffed toys, an item of your clothing or a radio in his crate. When he is left with items to play with, he won't feel alone, and they will keep him occupied while you are away.

If you adopt an adult Cairn Terrier who has not been socialized properly, you may find that his separation anxiety lasts a lot longer than normal. You will know that your adult Cairn Terrier is suffering from separation anxiety, if he exhibits the following symptoms:

- Loud continuous barking, crying or howling when you leave the house or the room.
- Biting, clawing, and scratching at windows or doors when you leave the house.
- He won't go outside alone, when you are home.
- Will not allow you to go anywhere alone, if he is shut out of the room you are in, he will sit and whine or cry, until you open the door.
- Over-excited greetings, even if you leave him for just two minutes.

How To Handle Separation Anxiety?

If your dog is suffering from mild to moderate separation anxiety, there are some simple techniques you can use to help him get over it:

- Provide your dog with an old item of clothing that has your scent on it.
- Delay greeting your dog when you come back home; wait for a few minutes, and even if you want to, don't give him an extended greeting.
- Practice leaving the dog for short periods of time, slowly extend the time away, until he gets used to you not being there.
- Leave a raw knuckle bone or his favorite toy for him to chew on or play with. Only leave him with a bone if his play area is outside the house, because this can become messy.
- Act as if you are about to leave, by picking up your keys and putting on your coat, and then sit back down. Eventually, your dog will not become so anxious when you are leaving the house.
- Give your dog a signal that you are going to return, such as leaving on the TV or radio, or by saying the words "I'll be back."

Once you can leave your dog for 30 minutes or more without him displaying signs of separation anxiety, you know he has overcome it. However, if these strategies don't work, or he is suffering from advanced separation anxiety, you will need to call in a trained professional to assist you.

Do Cairn Terriers Make Good Guard Dogs?

Cairn terriers are not big enough to be guard dogs; however, they do make good watchdogs. Because they were born and bred to hunt, they have very strong prey instincts and so the slightest of movements from something suspicious will cause them to bark. The Cairn Terrier is a fearless breed, and will protect its territory against anything that attempts to infiltrate it.

Are Cairn Terriers Good Pets?

This question depends on what you consider good. Cairn Terriers are very friendly dogs and affectionate dogs; however, they also have a rebellious streak. They can be very independent and refuse to listen to their owner. If you can handle this aspect of their character coupled with regular dog mischief, then yes, Cairn Terriers make very good pets.

CHAPTER 3

Cairn Terrier Breeders: What to Look For and What Should You Avoid?

I F you want a healthy purebred Cairn Terrier puppy, your best option is to look for a reputable breeder who is dedicated to raising dogs to the highest standards. Since the Cairn Terrier is recognized by the American Kennel Club, you can find a breeder through the national breed association.

Cairn Terrier Price – How Much Should I Expect To Pay?

Cairn terriers cost more from a breeder for several reasons; they are as follows:

- The potential parents of the puppies are checked for health issues such as hip, eye, and heart problems. If they don't meet the standards, they are not bred.

- They breed for temperament; your dog won't have behavioral problems because parents with a bad temperament are not selected for the breeding process.

- The health and behavior of a puppy has been checked for up to five generations.

- A reputable breeder will ensure that the puppy has been socialized, they are generally comfortable with traffic and household noises, and might even know some basic training commands.

- Some breeders provide genetic health testing to ensure that their puppies will not suffer from any inherited diseases later down the line.

- In the United States, purchasing a Cairn Terrier from a breeder will cost between $400 to $600.

- In Canada, purchasing a Cairn Terrier from a breeder will cost between $350 to $700.

- In the United Kingdom, purchasing a Cairn Terrier from a breeder will cost between £200 to £600.

Questions To Ask a Breeder?

- Do they have a contract to purchase that provides a transparent guarantee of the health of the puppy, and instructions regarding their refund policy?

- How well does the breeder know the parents of the puppy?

- Can they provide the family history of the puppy dating back several generations?

- Is the kennel well maintained, clean, and animal friendly?

- Will they allow you to see the other dogs in the kennel?

- Is there a limit placed on how you can handle the puppies?

- Is the breeder recognized by the national, state, or local breed club or organization?

- How often does the breeder pair the adult male and females together to breed?

What To Look Out For When You Visit a Breeder?

You should have a happy and positive experience when you visit a breeder. If you have a gut feeling that something is not quite right, it is best to follow your instincts and walk away. If you suspect that a breeder might be engaging in irresponsible breeding or puppy farming, don't make your purchase from them. You may feel as if you are saving the puppy from harm, but what you are doing by handing over your money, is enabling them to continue their unethical operation, and put even more dogs at risk.

When Not To Buy From a Breeder

- Do not buy a Cairn Terrier puppy during the Christmas season; responsible breeders don't sell during this time.
- Do not pick up the puppy from any other location, other than the breeders' premises.
- Do not buy from a breeder who won't allow you to watch a puppy interact with its mother.

Breeders You Should Not Trust

- A puppy farmer will tell you they can get you any sex or color you want, do not buy from them.
- Do not buy from a breeder who doesn't have significant knowledge about the Cairn Terrier.
- Do not buy from breeders who don't get along with their puppies.

- Do not buy from breeders if the mother and the puppy don't appear happy.
- Do not trust a breeder who says you can buy the puppy the first time you see him.
- Do not trust a breeder who doesn't ask about your lifestyle and how you intend on taking care of the puppy.

What The Breeder Will Expect From You?

A respectable Cairn Terrier breeder will want to ensure the health and safety of his puppies. There is a chance that he might not allow people to handle the puppies even if they are serious buyers. Whether you are enquiring or wanting to make a purchase, you may only be allowed to interact with the puppies from a distance. If they do allow you into the kennel to handle the dogs, there will be several restrictions in place. Here are some of the questions a breeder might ask you:

- What type of home do you have? How big is your yard? The breeder might ask to come and visit your residence to ensure that it is suitable for his puppy.
- Why are you buying the dog? Do you intend on breeding it?
- Do you have any other pets? Have you trained dogs in the past?
- You may have to sign a contract agreeing to train the dog properly.
- The breeder might require that you use a particular method to train the dog.
- Do you have any children? How many people will be interacting with the dog?

- If things don't work out, the breeder might request that you bring the dog back to them, instead of selling it.

The more information you and the breeder know about each other, the smoother the transaction will be. If you have got any concerns or issues, you should take your time to express them to the breeder. Don't go with the first breeder you meet, make sure you do some research before making a final decision. It is also a good idea to attend events and dog shows to give you a better idea of the type of breeder you would like to work with.

CHAPTER 4

Cairn Terrier Puppies For Sale: Where Is The Best Place To Find a Cairn Terrier For Sale?

Where ever you choose to buy your Cairn Terrier puppy, you want to make sure that it is from a reputable source. It is important that your focus is not on finding the cheapest option, because you will end up paying more in the long run.

Cairn Terrier Puppies For Sale Near Me - How Can I Find Cairn Terriers For Sale In My Local Area?

Breeders: Buying from a responsible breeder is the most expensive option, but it is also the most reliable. Most breeders will advise you to visit the litter a few times before deciding on the right puppy for you. They will often recommend a vet in your area, give you information about the food he will need to eat, trainers, let you know about any issues with the breed, as well as other things you might want to know about. Most breeders will also discuss issues with neutering or spaying the dog unless you want the puppy for future breeding stock or to become a show dog.

*Make sure you buy your Cairn Terrier from a reputable source, or you
risk experiencing health and other problems with your dog in the future.*

Before choosing a breeder, check that the Kennel Club in your
area recognizes the breeder. Ask about events or shows the
breeder has participated in. If the breeder has a problem with
providing this information, you might want to think about
looking for another breeder.

Rescue Shelters: Puppies are often abandoned when owners
realize that it is either too expensive, or too time consuming,
to raise a puppy. These puppies are left without homes and
taken into rescue centers. They will vaccinate, treat for parasites,
microchip, socialize, and if necessary, neuter puppies before
advertising them for adoption.

Cairn Terrier Adults For Sale: Where Is The Best Place To Find Cairn Terrier Adults For Sale?

Rescue shelters are great places to find adult Cairn Terriers. They will allow you to spend time with the dog so that you can get to know him, before adopting him. Adults are different from puppies, they have already been trained and socialized which can either be a positive or a negative, depending on the character of the dog. An adult Cairn who has already been trained or socialized knows how to behave, they are housetrained, toilet trained, and they know how to act around people. This means that you won't have much training to do, getting him used to your way of doing things won't be too hard.

The downside of buying an adult Cairn Terrier is that they may exhibit behaviors that their previous owner allowed them to get away with, but that you don't like. Even though you won't need to spend too much time training him, your time and money might be spent dealing with his age-related issues such as sight and hearing loss, and other health-related problems.

Shelters will often agree to take the dog back if things don't work out, and he doesn't adapt well to his new environment. This means that you won't have to worry about trying to find another owner.

When buying a Cairn Terrier from a rescue shelter, make sure you ask the right questions and get as much information as possible, before you buy the dog.

- Has the dog had a full checkup? Are his vaccinations up to date?
- Does the dog have any behavioral problems such as excessive barking or eating?

- Does the dog appear to be energetic and healthy?
- Will you be able to spend time getting to know the dog, before taking him home?
- What is the policy on neutering or spaying the dog?
- Can you bring the dog back to the shelter if he doesn't adapt well to your home and family?

The Bad Side Of Adopting a Dog From a Rescue Shelter

- There is not much choice over the breeding, gender, and size of the dogs available.
- There is limited information about their medical history and lineage.
- Most dogs will have to be neutered before they leave the shelter, or you will have to make an agreement to spay or neuter the dog.

Pet Stores: Regardless of the country, pet stores sell their dogs at similar prices to breeders. The only negative about purchasing from a pet store is that the dogs are not championship quality, you might not be able to see them due to behavioral or physical problems, and they are typically purchased from puppy mills or other nefarious sources, where there has been no regard for the health of the puppies or breeding stock.

One of the conditions for a Cairn Terrier breeder to join an association to prove their legitimacy is that they don't sell puppies to pet stores. So even though pet stores may sell Cairn Terriers at a similar price to breeders, they don't come with the same guarantees.

CHAPTER 5

Cairn Terrier Colors and Mixes: What Should You Expect?

You will be spoilt for choice when choosing your Cairn Terrier because they come in a wide variety of colors and mixes.

Cairn Terrier Colors – What Colors Do Cairn Terriers Come In?

Black Cairn Terrier: Black Cairn Terriers are simply black, there is no color variation.

Red Brindle Cairn Terrier: The word brindle means a tawny or brownish color with streaks of another color running through it. So, the red brindle is a mixture of red and brown, with streaks of another color running through it. The red can come in a flame, or bright auburn color.

Wheaten Cairn Terrier Mix: Wheaten is a color similar to wheat, a pale yellow-beige color.

Brindle Cairn Terrier: As stated, the word brindle means a tawny or brownish color with streaks of another color running through it.

There is no shortage of colors and mixes with the Cairn Terrier.

Grey Haired Cairn Terrier: There are many different shades of gray; this coat ranges from a very pale, nearly white color to a dark, steel, deep gray that can be mistaken for black. Gray can also be a mixture of black and white that looks gray because of how close the two colors are to each other.

Cream Haired Cairn Terrier: There are very light and very dark cream-colored Cairn Terriers. There is also a variation of colors in between. The very light-colored cream Cairns are often mistaken as white, but there are no white Cairn Terriers.

Cairn Terrier Mixes – What Mixes Do Cairn Terriers Come In?

Cairn Terrier Poodle Mix: Also known as the Poocan, Cairnpoodle, Cairnpoo, and Cairnoodle; it is a cross between a poodle and a purebred Cairn Terrier. Despite his independent nature, the dog is easy to train and is very eager to please. Cairnoodles enjoy entertaining people, so as well as obedience training, you can also train him to perform funny tricks.

This dog is loving, devoted, and social. His character is combined with that of the bold cairn terrier and the sensitive poodle.

The Cairn Terrier Poodle Mix is considered to be a hybrid breed; therefore, it is not recognized by the American Kennel Club. However, it is recognized by the International Designer Canine Registry, the Dog Registry of America, the Designer Dogs Kennel Club, and the American Canine Hybrid Club.

Cairn Terrier Corgi Mix: The Cairn Terrier Corgi Mix is also known as the Cairn Corgi. It is a cross between the Welsh Corgi and the Cairn Terrier. Depending on the dominant traits of the parents, the Cairn Corgi will resemble either parent. If it looks like the Cairn Terrier, it will have a square-shaped muzzle and head with medium-sized ears that fold downwards. If the breed resembles the Welsh Corgi, it will have a thinner muzzle and a round head. The ears are either erect and pointed or erect and rounded, depending on the breed of the Corgi.

The body of the Cairn Corgi is long, it gets this trait from the Welsh Corgi, but it won't be as long as the pure-bred corgi.

The Cairn Terrier Corgi Mix is not hypoallergenic, and it does shed moderately. It has got medium length hair that requires daily brushing to keep it from matting, tangling and to get rid of the debris and dirt that sticks to the coat. If the Cairn Corgi looks like the Welsh Corgi, he is much more difficult to train.

Unlike the purebred Cairn Terrier, this breed rarely barks, unless it needs something.

It is recognized by the Dog Registry of America, and the American Canine Hybrid Club.

Cairn Terrier Australian Shepherd Mix: The Cairn Terrier Australian Shepherd Mix is also known as the Shepterrier. It is a cross between the Australian Shepherd and the Cairn Terrier. The breed is a medium-sized breed and will look more like an Australian Shepherd, it also has the same blue, amber, yellow to dark eye color as the Australian Shepherd.

The Shepterrier is more sensitive than the Australian Shepherd, and because of the nature of both parent dogs, they either dislike, are indifferent towards or tolerate other pets. The Australian Shepherd has a lot of energy, and requires high intensity exercise every day. Although the Cairn Terrier also has a lot of energy and requires daily exercise, their intensity level is not that high. The Shepterrier has a lot of energy, and requires daily exercise.

This breed is not suited to living in an apartment, they need plenty of space to run around.

Cairn Terrier King Cavrin Mix: The Cairn Terrier King Cavrin, also known as the King Cavrin Spaniel, and the King Cavrin is a cross between the Cairn Terrier and the King Charles Spaniel. It can take on the look of either parent; its coat can either be silky or short, long, rough and harsh, fine or dense. It can have small, pretty eyes with a recognizable expression, or medium sized hazel or dark eyes with a keen expression. The ears are either small, long, silky and feathered or erect, small and pointed. The tail is typically docked and high up, or short. The body shape is almost square like and well proportioned. The King Cavrin comes in a variety of colors, sand, gray, black, brindle, red, solid ruby, black and tan, Blenheim, or tricolor.

This breed may or may not be hypoallergenic, and will be a minimal to moderate shedder. He is a happy, affectionate and loving dog, who socializes well with people of all ages. He is also very energetic, intelligent, and eager to please his owner. They are fast learners and will require daily exercise to burn off their energy.

CHAPTER 6

Bringing Your Cairn Terrier Home: What Should I Consider?

O nce your puppy has been chosen, you will need to prepare your home before he arrives. There are several things that must be taken care of to make the transition to his new environment as comfortable as possible.

Cairn Terriers are hyperactive and energetic dogs, as much as you would like them to, they are not going to sit in a corner all day, they are going to explore their new environment. There is nothing wrong with your new puppy wanting to become familiar with his new home, but he has not been housetrained yet, so if you want to keep your abode in one piece, you will need to confine him.

Cairn Terrier Accessories – What Type Of Accessories Will I Need?

- Puppy or baby gates for the stairs and doors
- Plenty of toys including high-quality chews. Your puppy will start teething between the ages of 3 and 8 months

- A play-pen: It should be big enough for your puppy to play in
- A grooming glove
- A soft bristle brush or a slicker brush
- A toothpaste, and toothbrush, specifically for dogs
- Nail clippers
- Scissors with rounded ends
- Dog shampoo and conditioner
- A water and food dish: It should be skid proof and heavy. Buy separate dishes because they are easier to keep clean.
- A harness or a dog collar
- A dog bed
- A dog crate for the home and car
- Baby blankets for the crates and bed
- A few sturdy dog leads

Cairn Terrier Harness - What Type Of Cairn Terrier Harness Will I Need?

Cairn Terriers are feisty and energetic dogs, even when they are on a leash, they will attempt to run off. To control this behavior, not only will you need to train him, but you will also need a sturdy harness, to attach the leash to.

Cairn Terrier Kennels - What Type Of Kennel Should I Buy For My Cairn Terrier?

A dog kennel is also known as a dog cage or a crate; it is designed to be a safe and secure area that the dog can relax in when it needs to.

It is typically made from a wireframe with a removable tray inside the base, for his bedding. A kennel is available in a range of designs, sizes, and materials.

A dog kennel has four main uses:

- **Training Aid**: To help with toilet training or to get them used to being on their own.
- **Transportation:** Kennels help to keep dogs comfortable and secure when traveling.
- **Veterinary Advised:** A vet may suggest that a kennel is used in certain circumstances; for example, to recover from surgery.
- **Short-Term Confinement:** When the owner has to leave the dog in the house for a short period of time.

The type of kennel you should get will depend on the size and the needs of your Cairn Terrier.

Cairn Terrier Environment - Adapting Your Home For Your Cairn Terrier

If you have a loud house, you might want to practice being quiet a few weeks before you bring your puppy home. Puppies find it difficult to tolerate noise, it makes them nervous. So, keep the excitement levels to a minimum, and keep the TV and music on a low volume. You will also need to do the following:

- Baby gates: For safety reasons, you will need to restrict access to the stairs, until he is big enough to maneuver them safely.
- House plants: Remove all houseplants from his reach, not only are many of them highly toxic, but you will have a big mess to clean up when he knocks them down!

- Dangling items: As stated, Cairn Terriers are hyperactive and energetic, and if they see an opportunity to jump up and get something, they will. Therefore, remove all dangling items from drapes, furniture, and other fixtures. Take extra precautions with electrical wires because your puppy will chew on them. Avoid choking hazards with items such as drapery pulls, make sure they are securely attached to a wall, or that they are high enough that your Cairn Terrier is unable to reach them.

- Remove all temptation: Puppies like to chew on things, if you want to keep your most prized possessions in one piece, keep them out of your Cairn Terriers reach. Such items might include cell phones, remote controls, valuable ornaments, furniture and your children's toys.

What Happens On Pick Up Day?

A puppy is like a baby, it is a new and exciting addition to the family, but when you get to the location where you will collect the puppy, try and contain your enthusiasm, or you will scare him. Bring a plastic kennel or a crate lined with a soft blanket or liner, some chew toys, and an old t-shirt that has your scent on it. The idea is to create a den-like environment for the dog.

Put the puppy into the crate and shut the door, secure it to the car by fastening it with the seatbelt. Find out from the person you have made the purchase from whether the dog has used the bathroom or eaten, because you don't want him to have to use the toilet during the journey home. If you have a long drive, don't worry if your new Cairn Terrier starts to whine and cry, this is normal, he is not used to you and neither is he used to being cooped up in a car for long periods of time. If you make your purchase from a breeder and you let them know in advance that you will have a long journey home, they may sedate the puppy. However, this is completely up to you. If you do choose this option, make sure that you monitor him throughout the journey.

If you have a family, it is advised that only one or two people go and collect the puppy. This might be disappointing for the kids, but you don't want to put too much pressure on your puppy. Too many people in his space at one time, will stress him out. You want to create a quiet and peaceful atmosphere for the dog to make the event as positive as possible.

When you get to your house, take your puppy outside on a long leash or monitor him closely in a fenced yard. If he goes to the toilet while outside, praise him immediately, as this is a great way to start the bonding process.

The breeder should have given you information about his feeding routine, it is best to stick to this routine, at the beginning. You can slowly start changing the routine to suit your schedule later. Make sure the food is the same as what he is used to eating; you can also change this at a later date.

Your puppy is going to be nervous, he is in a new environment with faces he doesn't recognize, so try and keep the excitement to a minimum, to avoid causing him any stress. Put your puppy in his new area and allow him to explore it; at this point, he might start crying. You are going to feel sorry for him and want to pick him up and pamper him, but this is not a good idea because it will encourage negative behavior. Instead, comfort him by placing a well-secured hot water bottle, a used piece of clothing, or a radio playing softly in the area. Interaction and petting with your puppy should only take place when he is quiet. When he is crying and whining, ignore him. This might sound harsh, but if you pamper him when he cries, he will take advantage of you and start whining every time he wants attention, knowing that you will give it to him. However, if you ignore him, he will soon learn that the best way to get attention, is to be quiet.

Introduction Time - Introducing Your Cairn Terrier To Friends And Family

It's important to socialize your dog as early as possible; however, you also need to remember that he is going to be nervous because he is in a new environment around people he has never seen before. Don't overwhelm him by bringing all your friends over at once, introduce them slowly and let him get to know each person before you introduce him to another friend.

Your Cairn will need to get used to the people he is living with; however, introductions should be a slow and gentle process.

Cairn Terrier Puppies and Children - Will My Cairn Terrier Get On With My Children?

Cairn Terriers love children; however, because of their bold nature, you will need to operate with a firm hand to make sure they do not cause any unintended harm. Also, because they are hunters of small game, their prey/chase instinct is highly developed; so, when children scream and run around, a Cairn Terrier is likely to give chase. This is often mistaken as aggression. You will also need to teach your children how to act with the puppy because what children consider playing, such as tugging on his whiskers and tail, is threatening to a Cairn Terrier and they may react by defending themselves. It is also important to note that younger children might be afraid of the new puppy, if the child is holding the dog and it tries to escape or get frightened, this might scare your child. To avoid this, spend some time teaching your children the right way to handle the puppy, and what to do if the puppy does something naughty. The golden rule is not to leave young children alone with your Cairn Terrier.

The Cairn Rescue League will not house a Cairn in a home with children, unless they know that the dog is well behaved around kids.

Cairn Terrier Puppies and Cats - Will My Cairn Terrier Get Along With My Cat?

Cairn Terriers get along with cats inside the home, but they have a tendency to fight with cats outside the home. Unless a Cairn Terrier is known to get along with cats, the Cairn Rescue League will not place a Cairn in a home with cats.

CHAPTER 7

Feeding Your Cairn Terrier: What's Essential?

You will need to feed your Cairn Terrier puppy often until it is between the ages of six to eight months old. Feed puppies under four months old four small meals a day, and puppies between the age of four to eight months three times per day. When he is older than eight months, reduce feeding to twice a day, but you will still need to monitor the amount of food he eats. Give your puppy 10 to 20 minutes to eat, then remove the food from the area. This will encourage your puppy to eat when food is given to him, and it will also help with housetraining. When Cairns get too hungry, they feel sick and vomit. To prevent overeating, do not give your Cairn Terrier free access to food. Eating too much can cause obesity and make it difficult to potty train him.

Best Food For Cairn Terriers

To preserve the health of your puppy, invest in premium, high quality dry food. Avoid foods that contain synthetic preservatives such as BHT and BHA. You should also bear in mind that Cairns are prone to food allergens such as soy, wheat, and corn.

Dry food contains additional protein and nutrients required for a growing Cairn Terrier puppy. When purchasing his food, read the label, and make sure that the first items on the ingredients list are fishmeal, meat, or grains. Avoid foods that are high in cornmeal as the first ingredient. Such foods are cheaper, but the nutritional content is poor, and it will cause your dog to go to the toilet more during the day. Wet foods do not always have the correct nutritional balance and are known to cause digestive issues in Cairn Terrier puppies. It is also harder to measure wet foods based on caloric and protein content, which can lead to your puppy either getting too much or not enough food. Be sure that you measure the food given to your puppy and stick to the recommended portions according to his weight.

If you want to give him a treat, buy dog cookies from the store, or make your own. It is also important to note that Cairn Terriers should not consume more than five percent of their total food intake in treats, per day. Your dog will quickly gain weight if you feed him too many treats. It will also reinforce the bad habit of preferring treats instead of normal food.

When your Cairn Terrier puppy is chewing on a bone, make sure he is monitored carefully, to avoid choking. Only feed joint or knucklebones, and take it from him when it gets small enough to swallow or when it starts to splinter.

Provide your puppy with fresh water throughout the day; don't give him tap water, instead let him drink filtered, or contaminant-free bottled water.

Holistic Diet For a Cairn Terrier

Dogs are no different from humans when it comes to diet. Feed them healthy nutritious food, and they will live a disease-free life. Feed them processed junk food, and you will spend the majority of your time and money taking your Cairn Terrier to the vet for medical treatment. Dogs are susceptible to cancer, digestive issues, diabetes and arthritis, which are all conditions that have their roots in a bad diet. There are some genetic diseases, but they are rare. If you want to see your Cairn Terrier live into his golden years, a holistic diet is your best option.

The word "holistic" means to treat the whole person as opposed to just getting rid of the symptoms. For example, if your dog starts to experience dry and flaky hair there are a range of shampoos promising to correct the problem. They may make your dog's hair shiny and smooth again, but the underlying issue has not been resolved, which means it will come back at a later date.

It may be that your dog is allergic to coloring, a filler, or ingredients in his food. Or he might be lacking in important nutrients, such as omega 3 fatty acids. Regardless of the issue, a holistic diet will tackle the problem from the root.

Holistic food is made out of high-quality ingredients such as digestive enzymes, probiotics, vitamins, antioxidants, real meat, whole grain rice, omega 3 fatty acids and other healthy nutrients, all of which help to keep your dog's body functioning at its best.

In the first few weeks of feeding your Cairn Terrier holistic foods, you will notice that his energy levels will increase, his hair will look shiny and healthy, his digestive system will be more effective, and much more.

Foods Not To Feed Your Cairn Terrier

Don't feed your Cairn Terrier human food, they can be very dangerous, even to the point of death. Human foods that can cause the most damage include:

- Raw pork
- Raw fish
- Raw chicken
- Nuts such as macadamia and walnuts
- Chocolate
- Mushrooms
- Onions
- Garlic
- Alcohol
- Raisins

Do Cairn Terriers Like Water?

Cairn Terriers love water, they like drinking it to quench their thirst, but they also enjoy swimming and playing in it and going to the beach.

Cairn terriers love the water, just make sure to supervise them!

CHAPTER 8

Cairn Terrier Training: How Can You Train a Cairn Terrier Easily While Having Fun?

Training your Cairn Terrier can be the most difficult or exciting time in the life of your dog ownership. Cairn Terriers are extremely stubborn dogs, and some owners can become frustrated with their sassy attitudes. Therefore, the aim in this chapter is to ensure that training your puppy is fun and exciting, for the both of you.

Training Items You Might Need

- Treats
- Target stick
- Clicker
- Portable mat
- Collar and harness
- Leashes
- Long line
- Barriers

Making Training Fun

Some owners dread training their puppies and would rather pay to have a professional take over the responsibility. However, this doesn't have to be the case, training your puppy can be as fun as you want it to be.

To begin, make sure you are in the right mood, dogs are very sensitive to emotions and will detect if you are angry, tired or frustrated; this will make the training session unpleasant for the both of you.

Providing your puppy with lots of treats, verbal praise and hugs will make your puppy want to participate in training sessions. After a good session, have some play time as well, this will also provide an incentive for him to do well during training.

In addition, allow your Cairn to exercise prior to training him. This will give your dog the opportunity to burn off excess energy, so that he can focus better. If this energy is not released, he will be more interested in running around and playing, instead of training.

All puppies enjoy spending time with their owners, learning and being praised. They will look forward to training sessions if they are conducted in a positive and pleasant environment where your puppy feels as if he has accomplished something.

Consistency Is Key

This is one of the most important aspects of training. Your puppy will find it very difficult to grasp basic concepts if they are not continuously reinforced or if expectations are constantly changing. If you live with a family, it is important that everyone is on the same page, and you are all teaching him the same things. For example, if one person is giving your puppy the command "down," and another person is saying "sit," he is going to get confused. Keep commands consistent and simple.

In addition to the language used for commands, it's also important to make sure that everyone in your home expects the same from your dog. For example, your children might like the puppy to sleep in the bed with them, but you expect him to sleep in his crate. Again, this type of inconsistency will confuse your puppy, and it will take longer to learn what is required of him.

Write out a list of commands and expectations set out for the dog and give them to each person living in the house. Have a meeting and explain why it's imperative that they follow them. If you are taking your puppy to a training class, take the whole family with you so they can observe how training is initiated.

Patience Is Key

Puppies are like toddlers; it's going to take them a while before they get it right. Before a child learns to walk, they fall countless times before they are stable on their feet. Would you punish a child for not getting it right the first couple of times? I am hoping you have answered no to this question! You are going to be patient with him, and praise him for his efforts. You should apply the same principle to your puppy.

Housebreaking is the first lesson you should teach your Cairn, but it is also the most difficult. So, you will need to allocate plenty of time and energy to this.

Get Into a Routine

As you are probably aware, children need a consistent routine, because it provides discipline and structure in their lives. As you do with your own kids, or if you don't have children, you remember when you were a child, children are told what time to wake up, what time to go to bed, when to eat dinner, what time to do their homework and when they are allowed to play with friends. Life without routine leads to anxiety, stress, and a feeling of being overwhelmed. The same is true in a dog's life.

Dogs are creatures of habit, their response to the world around them is dependent upon how they feel and how satisfied they are with their environment. For a dog to look at the world through positive eyes, and feel comfortable with change, dogs must have a stable routine that they are established and grounded in. A consistent routine means that they know what to expect from their owners and from life, and this sense of stability will show in their behavior.

Dogs that do not have an established routine feel insecure, anxious, stressed and depressed about the inconsistency in their lives. These feelings will cause them to act out in negative ways, and this can also influence their physical health.

A consistent training routine will make it easier for your dog to remember what is required of him. Repetition is another important aspect of the training process, and if he is continuously repeating what is required of him, it will accelerate the learning process.

Dog Training Basics

The basic commands that every dog should know how to respond to are the following:

- Sit
- Come
- Down
- Stay

Training Your Cairn Terrier To Sit

It is natural for your dog to want to sit down, so use this to your advantage during training.

- Pay attention to your dog and take note when he is about to sit down. At that point, say "Sit." This will teach your Cairn that sit means to put his bottom on the ground.
- You can also use treats to encourage him to sit.
- Sit on the floor with your puppy, hold the treat above his head, and move it slightly backwards. The puppy will lift its nose up towards the treat and move his head back. This will cause him to sit down.
- As soon as his back quarters start lowering, say "Sit," when his bottom is on the floor, give him the treat.

These sessions should be short, he shouldn't sit more than five times during training. Mix the come and sit commands to keep your Cairn thinking.

Praise him each time he sits, once he has mastered the command, slowly stop giving him the treats, and give him more verbal praise.

Training Your Cairn Terrier To Come

The "come" command is one of the most important instructions for a dog to learn. Not only does it provide your dog with safety barriers, but it also gives him more freedom. Once he has a clear understanding of this command, you can allow him to take walks off-leash in appropriate and safe locations, without worrying that he will take off running, and ignore you when you call him.

The first step in getting your puppy to understand the come command, is to understand why he might decide that he doesn't want to come. Maybe he is too engrossed in the current activity he is taking part in, or maybe he doesn't feel like interacting with anyone and wants to spend time alone. Also, dogs like their freedom, if there is one thing they can't stand, it's being constrained by a leash. A dog will quickly learn that when they are walking around leash-free, and their owner calls, there is a high chance they are getting the leash. Since this is something they detest, it is another reason why they will not come when being called.

To ensure that this behavior does not become a habit, it is important to keep your Cairn on a leash, when out in the training area.

The easiest way to teach a Cairn to come, is by using food as an incentive. This method works best when the dog is slightly hungry. So, it is important that you choose the right time to train him, but you should also make sure that you don't give him too many treats, or he won't eat a proper meal, later.

Training periods should take place over short periods, several times throughout the day. Don't train your dog during times of stress, or as soon as he has finished eating. Remember to give him lots of attention through praise and petting when he gets it right.

Once he has gained a full understanding of the command, start adding distractions. If you are training him outside, keep your Cairn on a leash, and be firm but gentle.

To start the training session, make sure you have got your puppy's undivided attention, and that there are no distractions in the area. To begin with, you will only need to be a few feet away from the dog, you can increase the distance, once he has mastered the command.

- Call the puppy by name; for example, if his name is Sooty, say "Sooty, come," or "Come Sooty!"
- Show him the treat.
- When he moves towards you, reward the puppy by giving him the treat.
- At the same time as giving him the treat, give him lots of praise and petting.
- Keep moving further back, while giving the command.
- Once your Cairn is coming immediately and consistently, slowly start eliminating the treats, and give him praise only.

Training Your Cairn Terrier To Lie Down

The "down" command can be taught in a similar way to the sit command.

- Make your dog sit, and then put the food in front of the dog on the ground. This should encourage him to lie on his stomach.
- If he stands up or doesn't respond to the command, gently move his front legs out at the same time, as giving the down command.
- When your Cairn lies down, reward him immediately with food and praise.
- Your puppy will then stand up ready for the next round. Continue to do this until he has a full understanding of the down command.
- Encourage him to lie down for longer periods, by waiting before giving him the reward and petting the puppy while he is on the ground.

As you did with the sit command, pay attention to when the dog is about to lie down naturally and give the command to lie down.

Training Your Cairn Terrier To Stay

Once he has learned to sit, come, and lie down, you should then teach him how to stay. Your dog will find it difficult to understand this command because Cairn Terriers are active dogs, and don't like standing still. Also, he will naturally want to follow you.

- Start by giving him the down command.
- Say "Stay," at the same time as putting your hand up, with your palm facing him.
- Take a step back and reward him, even if he stays still for one second.
- Slowly increase the space that you step back, and the time you want him to stay.

- If your cairn walks towards you instead of staying, don't punish him for disobeying the command. It is a natural part of the training process; he will eventually gain a full understanding of the command.

Training Your Cairn Terrier How To Walk On a Leash

Your Cairn Terrier is not going to like the leash, the best way to prevent bad behavior when he has it on, is not to allow it from the start. Use a collar with soft fabric and a buckle for adjustments. Make sure that the collar is a good fit, you should be able to place two fingers between the collar and his neck. If the collar is too tight, your dog will be uncomfortable and not want to wear it, if it is too loose, he will slip out of it. Don't use a choke style collar with your Cairn Terrier, and keep the puppy on a short leash, until he understands what it means to walk on a leash.

Start leash training in your back yard before taking him to a park or out on the streets. Also, it is easier for him to learn when there are fewer distractions, and he can give you his full attention.

- Use praise and treats to keep your Cairn walking in the same direction as you.
- If he starts pulling, give a quick tug on the leash and change direction.
- Do not pull or drag the puppy, you can also stop walking and wait until there is slack in the leash, before you start walking again.
- Stop and let your puppy work out when there is no more pressure on the leash. This will happen once he starts coming close to you.

Your puppy will soon learn that staying close to you when walking will keep the pressure off his neck, and he will start walking in the same direction and pace as you.

How To Housebreak Your Cairn Terrier

Before Cairn Terriers became household pets, they were hunting dogs, so they are easy to train, and they have a strong desire to please their owners. You will need to be consistent and firm to successfully housetrain your puppy. Remember, puppies are like children, they like structure and routine, but they will also push the boundaries to see how much they can get away with. You must let them know who's boss, from the get-go.

- Stand by the crate with your puppy and allow him to see you put one of his favorite toys or treats inside the crate. He is going to want to get his paws on the goodies and so will start moving towards it. At this point say, "Crate, Fido (use his name)," and allow him to walk into the crate. Keep the door open, if he wants to come back out, let him.

- When the puppy walks into the crate, praise him for doing so, don't say anything when he comes out.

- Close the door for a while, but pay attention to him, he will start to get restless, open the door before he starts whining. Again, don't praise him for leaving the crate.

- When your Cairn Terrier gets comfortable inside the crate with the door closed, walk away, but make sure the puppy can still see you. Keep increasing the length of time you move away from the crate. Once your puppy learns to remain calm inside the crate without you watching over him, you can start housetraining.

- Once he has been fed, crate him with a chew toy. Wait for 10-15 minutes and then take the puppy out of the crate to his potty, litter box, or outside toilet area. There should be no playful interaction during this time. Once the puppy has been to the toilet, praise him for his efforts. If he hasn't gone to the bathroom within five minutes, take him back to the crate, again, there should be no playful interaction during this time. Wait for five minutes, or until he starts getting agitated, and repeat the process.

- Before you go to bed, move the crate so that you can hear the puppy when he whines. Whining is an indication that he needs to use the bathroom, take him outside, but don't give him any attention, or he will start whining at night expecting you to play with him.

Your Cairn Terrier will start to see the crate as his private quarters, and he won't go to the toilet in it. If he does, it will be because you could not hear him when he needed to get out. Your puppy will never soil his crate out of rebellion, so don't punish him when he has an accident. If you are a first-time dog owner, think of your puppy as a baby, they don't have strong bladder or bowel muscles and find it difficult to hold their waste when they get the urge. Neither should you use the crate as a place of punishment, it's supposed to be a safe haven for him, somewhere he can relax, play, and take a nap. When your puppy starts associating it with punishment, he will refuse to go inside it when you need him to.

How To Discipline Your Cairn Terrier

As cute and adorable as your Cairn Terrier puppy might be, he is going to test your patience! Discipline is something you are going to have to incorporate into your training routine from the beginning if you want a well behaved and obedient dog. Your pup will have to learn to live amongst humans, dogs and humans have different ways of communicating, and your pup is not going to understand unless you teach him, so you are bound to bump heads occasionally.

Discipline will help your dog understand that his behavior is unacceptable, and that you are not going to tolerate it. Some naughty Cairn Terrier habits that you will need to punish him for include:

- Snatching food from the kitchen or dining table
- Destroying other people's items, by chewing them
- Going to the toilet inside the house, even after he has been trained
- Destroying the yard
- Barking late at night

These are some of the most common examples, but as his owner, you will know when he is acting up. To make training your Cairn Terrier easier, you are going to have to see things from his point of view. This means that you will need to learn to see the world through his eyes and understand his learning process.

Dogs don't generalize information

Your dog will understand the "sit" command at home because you have trained him to do so. He has practiced it, and you have rewarded and praised him for his obedience. However, you might not get the same response from your Cairn Terrier outside. This is because he has not been trained to do so in that environment, so he is not going to understand what is expected of him.

So why don't dogs generalize information? Dogs are associative learners, and the way they interpret information depends on the connection made between sensory cues and the event. These cues are typically visual and auditory, they pay attention to what you do through body language and hand gestures, or they pay attention to what you say. Also, the learning process is enforced by cause and effect. This is why rewarding your dog when he gets it right during training accelerates his willingness to obey. But when dogs decide how to respond to a command, they think back to the last time you made it. So, to combat this, you must remember that this is the first time you are giving him this command in this environment so you have to reward him for sitting outside, in the same way you would for sitting in the house.

If you are getting frustrated about why it appears that your Cairn Terrier obeys when he wants to, it is most likely a problem of generalization. Dogs are extremely intelligent creatures, but they may not display this unless they are given consistent training.

Generalizing behaviors is one of the most important aspects of training, but his disobedience may also be due to other factors such as how hungry or tired he is. So, you should always keep in mind that there are several aspects you should take into consideration.

It is also important to note that generalization is not only determined by environment, it might also include the following:

- **Training equipment:** Your Cairn Terrier will remember when you use a treat pouch or a clicker and associate them with obedience. So, it is important that these tools are slowly phased out of training, or that they are not visible to him when you give him a command.

- **Physical Position:** Dogs learn according to positioning; for example, if you ask your dog to sit while you are sitting next to him, he obeys, and you reward him, he might not obey the same command when you do so, standing in front of him. So, it is important that you practice the same command in different positions and angles. Be sure to repeat each variation several times until it becomes the norm to him.

- **Location:** Where you conduct your training will also determine his obedience. If you spend a week training him in the living room, and the next week switch to the bedroom, his response might be different. Also, the way the location is arranged can also determine his obedience. For instance, your Cairn Terrier might think he is in a totally different environment if you redecorate your living room. It is important to practice in several different locations and slowly increase the difficulty level. For example, you will experience more challenges training him in a busy park with lots of people and other dogs. But you will find it easier in a familiar location like your living room, where distractions are limited. However, your yard would be a nice middle ground, between these two extremes.

- Also, you can improve your dog's ability to learn in different environments by lowering the enforcement criteria, when training is taking place in a more challenging location. For example, if your puppy does not respond to the "sit" command in a busy park, you can make things easier for him by rewarding him for doing something such as making eye contact, when he hears your voice.

Finally, your Cairn Terrier will find it easier to generalize information over time. However, his obedience is determined by the amount of effort you put into training him at the same time as enforcing variation and repetition. The most difficult challenge when training your Cairn Terrier is committing to practice in real-world settings. This is essential if you want to ensure that your dog learns to obey you, no matter where he is.

Understanding Rewards

Rewards are essential when it comes to dog training, but it is important to understand that your puppy will respond more favorably to some rewards than others, so you must identify those which are of high value to him. Typically referred to as reward-based training, giving your dog a reward when he learns how to obey gives him the confidence he needs to thrive in a domestic environment. Also, as you and your dog grow to better understand each other's needs, reward-based training will solidify your bond.

Dogs are either food, toys, or praise motivated, so before you start being consistent with rewarding him, you will need to learn which one he responds to best. Some owners use rewards to bribe their dogs into quick obedience, but that is not the purpose of a reward. You should think of it as a wage given for doing a good job. If an employee doesn't turn up to work, he doesn't get paid, in the same way you don't reward your dog, if he doesn't respond favorably to your commands.

Intermittent Reinforcement

Don't give your Cairn Terrier a high-value reward all the time. For example, if your puppy responds most favorably to praise, give him food, or if he responds more favorably to toys, give him praise. Intermittent reinforcement gives your dog the motivation to quickly learn a command, in anticipation of the high-value reward.

Once your dog understands that he will get what he loves the most when he does what he is told, he will repeat this behavior because it is the quickest and easiest way to get what he wants, and it makes him feel good.

What Does It Mean To Discipline Your Cairn Terrier?

According to the Oxford Dictionary, the word discipline means: "The practice of training people to obey rules or a code of behavior, using punishment to correct disobedience." In other words, you can train your dog to obey the rules and codes of behavior you have set for him, through discipline.

One of the most important things to understand about discipline is that if you use it the wrong way, your dog might become aggressive. When you act out in anger and frustration, you will scare your puppy, he will quickly forget that you are his owner, and protect himself by attacking you. What you want is to build a bond with your dog based on mutual respect, you don't want him to start seeing you as his enemy.

You will need to be very patient with your Cairn Terrier; unlike humans, they don't do annoying things to spite you. They do them because they are dogs and don't know any better. For example, your dog might chew on your computer because he is teething, or out of boredom. So, when he does something that you don't like, before jumping to the conclusion that he is just being naughty, think about why he might be doing it instead. You can then solve the problem by:

- Taking him on more walks to make sure he isn't bored
- Buying him toys that are specifically for relieving teething pain
- Teaching him which items he can and cannot chew on

Discipline and Timing

Your Cairn Terrier will only respond to discipline when it is administered at the right time. For best results, you will need to intervene when he is in the middle of the act. Immediately after is also effective, but after more than a few seconds, your dog won't understand what he is being punished for.

No matter how frustrated you get with your dog, physical violence is unacceptable, and at no time should it be a part of your discipline program. Instead, use the following safe and effective methods to disrupt his negative behavior. As well as letting him know what he is doing wrong, you should also show him the right way to behave.

Five Ways To Discipline Your Cairn Terrier

Scruff-Shake: Take hold of the fur on his neck underneath his ear and give him a short quick shake. This works best when you catch him doing something bad.

Distract: Distract your puppy by making a loud noise when he is in the middle of the bad behavior. A slap on the table, or a loud yell will get him to stop what he is doing and focus on you.

Isolation: Puppies don't like being isolated, they love attention, and will hate it when you are not giving it to them. When your puppy does something you don't like, ignore him for a set period.

Put-Down: Reinforce that you are the boss, by gently pushing your puppy over onto his side or onto his back, and then standing over him.

Time out: Put the puppy outside for a couple of minutes, and then bring him back in and try again.

CHAPTER 9

Cairn Terrier Grooming: What Are the Secrets?

A s well as diet and exercise, grooming is an essential part of maintaining your puppy's health. Grooming your Cairn Terrier on a regular basis will reduce the risk of skin irritations, fleas, and other health problems. The good news is that Cairn Terriers are low maintenance dogs, and you won't need to do much to keep them looking good. Get your Terrier used to the grooming process by starting when he is a puppy.

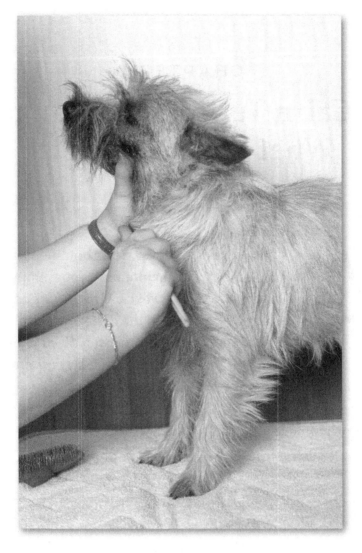

Start grooming your puppy early, so that he gets used to the process.

Cairn Terrier Shedding – Do Cairn Terriers Shed a Lot Of Hair?

Cairn Terriers do not shed a lot of hair, which is why you must comb their hair often to facilitate the shedding process.

How Often Should I Groom My Cairn Terrier?

Cairn Terriers have short hair, but it is also rough and wiry; therefore, you will need to groom them once a week. You should also give him a full grooming session once a month to keep his coat looking healthy.

Clipping His Hair

There are a variety of clippers on the market, but you might want to consider having this done at a professional groomer, instead of doing it yourself. Clipping is not an easy process, especially when you've got a dog as boisterous as a Cairn Terrier.

If you are brave enough to clip his hair yourself, make sure you get proper instructions, before you start. When using scissors to cut sensitive areas, make sure they have got rounded ends.

Choosing The Right Groomer

If you choose not to groom your dog at home, you can take him to a professional dog groomer. You don't want to put your dog through a traumatic grooming experience; therefore, make sure that you choose a reputable salon or individual, to groom your dog. Do some research and check out their online reviews and see what other people are saying about them. You can also ask friends and family members if they can recommend a groomer.

In the United Kingdom, the dog grooming industry is unregulated, but groomers registered with trade bodies such as the British Dog Groomers Association, and the Pet Care Trust are well qualified and more trustworthy than those that are not. In the United States it can vary by state. There are several factors you should consider, to help you to make the right choice.

- Ask your vet if they can recommend a groomer or a salon.

- Ask the groomer about their qualifications,

- Is the groomer concerned about whether your dog has been vaccinated, or if he is being treated for fleas or worms? This is important, because it helps to prevent the spread of infections, disease, and parasites.

- Ask for a tour of the premises, you want to make sure the place is clean enough to leave your dog there.

Cairn Terrier Grooming Tools – What Will I Need To Groom My Cairn Terrier?

There are many different brushes and grooming tools on the market, and it can get confusing when it comes to choosing the right ones. Some tools are going to work better on your Cairn Terrier than others, so it's a good idea to get some advice from your vet before investing in any equipment. In general, you will need the following tools to groom your dog:

- Stripping knife
- Scissors
- Pin brush
- Paper towels
- Nail clippers
- Dog shampoo
- Ear cleaning solution
- Double-sided dental tool
- Cotton balls
- Coat conditioner

Cairn Terrier Grooming – How To Groom a Cairn Terrier at Home

Bathing: Bathing your puppy is the most important part of the grooming process, he might be cute, but no one likes a smelly dog! It is important to make the experience fun for your dog, so that he won't want to run and hide when its bath time.

Bath time allows you to give your dog a thorough inspection for any new rashes, scrapes, cuts, and fleas. This is also a great time to inspect his nails, to see if they need trimming.

If you don't wash, brush or comb your dog on a regular basis, he could get dandruff, and his hair will become matted. This is when the coat hair gets clumped together. Mats are difficult to remove, and depending on the severity, you might need to shave the area.

When giving your dog a bath, you want to avoid getting water in his ears, doing so can cause a bacterial infection. You can do this by placing cotton balls just inside the ear canal before putting him in the water. You also want to avoid getting water in his eyes, so sponge wash his head, instead of pouring water over it.

- Check for matts before putting your dog in the bath; detangle them first, before shampooing, or they will get worse.
- Line your bathtub with a non-slip mat, or if the weather is good, you can bathe him outside.
- Don't use human shampoo, it has different pH balance and will dry out your dog's hair. There are plenty of good dog shampoos to choose from.
- Pour lukewarm water over his fur, and then apply the shampoo.

- Massage the shampoo into the fur for a minimum of five minutes.
- Rinse the shampoo off and make sure you get it all out, any remains can cause skin irritation.
- Dry your dog with a towel, or if he is comfortable with it you can use a hair dryer, but make sure you put it on a cool setting

Dog Shampoo Cairn Terrier – What Type Of Shampoo Will I Need?

You will need a shampoo specifically designed for dogs with hard coats. Look for natural and organic ingredients where possible, and avoid harsh detergents. Also, look for a shampoo that is a natural color rather than a bright color, which usually indicates artificial coloring, which can be an irritant.

Cairn Terrier Nail Cutting

It is in your best interest to cut your Cairn Terriers nails; sharp nails can hurt you!

Cairn Terriers have strong nails, as you know they are hunter dogs, so they were designed to dig and to grip hold of uneven surfaces. As domestic pets, smooth surfaces and soft beds will not wear their nails down, which means it is even more important to trim them. Dogs' nails get sharper when they are left to grow, and can cause damage to human skin and your furniture. Additionally, long nails are not comfortable for your Cairn, it will cause your dog to put his weight on the back pad, instead of spreading it out evenly over the whole foot. Once your dog reaches his golden years, trimming their back nails becomes especially important.

The Structure Of a Dog's Nail

Canine nails are hollow, they are like the horn of a ram. The 'quick' lies inside the nail and contains a combination of nerves and blood supply. Clipping the nails removes any additional nail that grows past the quick. You must be extremely careful when cutting your dog's nails, because cutting the quick is very painful, and he will not trust you to cut his nails again. If this does happen, and the pain traumatizes him, a vet may need to put him under sedation any time his nails need trimming. On the other hand, trimming his nails can be a fun experience for both you and your terrier.

Nail Clippers

Nail clippers are the fastest way to cut your puppy's nails, but it is also the most dangerous. You can exercise more control and less trauma when using a clipper with one moving blade and a fixed end. If his nails are transparent and white, you can see where the quick finishes and easily cut your Cairn's nails using this method. On the other hand, if your dog has got dark-colored or black nails, you will find it difficult to locate where the quick finishes, and this is how accidents happen. If you choose to use this type of clipper, you will need to use the cutting action of the tool to file off the sharp edges of his nail.

Nail clippers with scissor action are the most difficult to use because they tend to squeeze the quick.

Filing

Filing is the safest way to trim your dog's nails. Place your dog in a position that's comfortable for the both of you, you can either do this by laying him on your lap, or using a grooming table. The best time to file his nails is when he is feeling relaxed lying on the couch, or snuggled up in front of the fire. A human file is perfect for small dogs.

Start by steadying the nail from behind, using your index finger or thumb. Use your other hand to file in an upwards motion, from underneath the nail. After around 20 strokes, touch the nail with your finger to check whether it feels soft. This method gives you full control of the trimming process, because you can stop immediately when the nail starts getting soft, if you draw blood, or when you get too close to the quick. The only downside to this method is that it is time-consuming and tedious.

The Digger Dog Nail File

This is an Australian invention and is a fairly new way of trimming dogs' nails. The aim of this method is to get him to file his own nails by rubbing them on an abrasive surface. Once his nails are at an acceptable length, either he will stop, or you can check to see whether they have been filed down enough. The digger dog nail file method is a fun and exciting way to trim his nails.

The device is made up of a small box with an abrasive surface over the top. It has a sliding door with a handle that covers a concealed space. You can place treats in the drawer, and when he starts digging, reveal the treat, and give him a reward. Do this several times so that your puppy understands that he is being rewarded for filing his nails. This is a quick way of trimming his nails, it is easier for you, and a great incentive for your dog to want to trim his nails.

Dremel – Electric Nail Grinders

These electronic grinders are made up of a stone grinding wheel. They are noisy machines, so you will need to train him to get used to the noise. Care and careful attention are essential when using this type of equipment, because it is easy to go too far and damage the quick. But if you can train your Cairn to cope with this, it is a very successful method. Breeders and professional dog groomers prefer this method. For the novice pet owner, there are specifically designed nail grinders with a slow spin and a protective case around the stone grinder.

Cairn Terriers Dental Care

Dental disease affects approximately 80 percent of dogs by the age of two. Unfortunately, Cairn Terriers are prone to dental conditions more so than other dogs. Once tartar builds up on the teeth, it starts affecting the roots of the teeth and the gums. If dental disease is not prevented or treated, your dog will lose his teeth, and risk damaging his joints, heart, liver and kidneys. At its worst, dental disease can cut your terrier's lifespan short by one to three years. Regular cleaning and dentist visits will keep your Cairn's teeth healthy for life.

Start by buying a toothbrush and toothpaste especially for dogs. It is important that you use dog toothpaste, because it is safe for him to swallow. Follow these steps to clean your terrier's teeth:

- Start slowly, after a few weeks he will start getting used to having his teeth cleaned
- Allow him to taste the toothpaste, it will condition your puppy to believe that brushing his teeth is a treat, and not another boring task
- Rub a soft cloth against his gums, to get him used to the feeling of having his mouth touched
- Once he gets used to the cloth, switch to a small brush that you put on your finger. This will help him to become familiar with the feeling of having his teeth brushed
- Once you feel that your dog is ready, graduate to a full-length toothbrush

As well as brushing his teeth, keep his mouth healthy by doing the following:

- Don't give him bones too often, prolonged chewing can damage his teeth
- Specialist foods and dental chews can help to keep his mouth healthy
- Limit his intake of sugary treats, it will cause a buildup of bacteria on his teeth
- Buy toys that clean the teeth while he is chewing on them

Bad Breath: If you notice that your dog's breath is not smelling very fresh, you might need to brush his teeth more often. There is also the possibility that there are other health issues:

- **Mouth tumor:** This is a rare condition, but as well as bad breath, do not ignore symptoms such as difficulty chewing and excessive drooling
- **Diabetes:** Fruity or sweet-smelling breath on your dog is a sign of diabetes
- **Kidney Disease:** If your dog's breath starts to smell like urine, he may have kidney disease
- **Something stuck in his teeth:** Trapped food can cause an overgrowth of bacteria, which will cause bad breath
- **Dental disease:** As well as bad breath, gum infections and rotten teeth are a sign of dental disease

Additionally, regardless of how healthy your Cairn's teeth are, have a professional check his teeth every six to 12 months. A normal checkup with your vet should include a routine dental examination, but check beforehand.

Cairn Terrier Ears – How To Clean The Ears Of Your Cairn Terrier

Cairn Terrier ears are small and upright which means they are not prone to ear infections. However, you will need to clean them on a regular basis, to ensure that they remain free from infection.

How often: Your vet will tell you how often you need to clean your Cairn's ears. In general, he will either need monthly, once every two weeks, or weekly cleaning. If he does get an ear infection, you will need to clean the ears daily at the same time as treating the infection with medication. Daily cleaning when there is an infection is important, because putting an ointment into the ear while it is clogged up with wax and dirt, will only make the infection worse.

Your dog's ears should always smell clean, a foul or a yeasty bread like smell is an indication of an infection, and you will need to take him to the vet immediately. Other signs of ear infection include:

• Discharge from the ear
• Shaking of the head
• Scratching the ears
• Red ears
• Inflamed ears
• Yelping or crying when you stroke his ears

If you are a first-time pet owner, you might feel nervous about cleaning his ears at home. If this is the case, you can take him to the vet or a dog groomer to have his ears cleaned, but this should not be a long-term solution because it can get expensive.

Here are some steps to clean your dog's ears at home:

• You will need gauze or cotton balls and an ear cleaner that has been approved by a vet. You can purchase them online, at a pet store or from your vet.
• If your dog's ears are dirty, the cleaning process will be messy, so you can either clean his ears while you are giving him a

bath, or secure a towel around his neck and chest with a clip. This will prevent the mess from his ears, as well as the cleaner from getting onto his coat.

• To start, squeeze a small amount of ear cleaner into the ear and let it roll down into the canal. Massage the base of the ear gently to activate the cleaner, so that it breaks down the debris and wax. At this time, you will need to encourage him to shake his head, but before he does so, wrap a towel around his head, so that the mess from his ears doesn't fly all over the place.

• Gently wipe the outside and the inside of the ear using a gauze square or a cotton ball. Use your finger to push down into the ear as far as possible but refrain from using cotton buds as this can be uncomfortable for your dog. You will know when his ears are clean when there is no more debris left on the gauze or cotton ball.

Plucking His Ear Hair: If there is a lot of hair growing in his ear canal, you might want to pluck it out, before starting the cleaning process. Again, if you are a first-time Cairn owner, and you are nervous about doing this, ask your vet or dog groomer to show you the correct way to pluck out the hairs. You can either pluck the hairs out with your fingers, or use hemostats, which are blunt-nosed tweezers.

If plucking your dog's ears cause irritation, wait for a few days before cleaning, to give them time to calm down, so that you don't cause additional irritation.

Cairn Terrier Coat – How Do I Keep The Coat Of My Cairn Terrier Immaculate?

As mentioned earlier, you will need to wash and clip your dog's hair, to keep it in good condition. Brushing and stripping your Cairn Terriers coat, will give it that extra sheen.

Using a pin brush, start brushing at the head, going against the direction that the hair is growing. This is what gives your dog its distinctive, fluffy, full head of hair. Brush against the grain for the rest of the body, work carefully so that you can loosen any loose hair from the undercoat. After the whole coat has been brushed in the opposite direction, smooth out the coat by brushing with the grain.

Strip off the dead long hairs from the outer coat. Start at the base of the back, take a small section of hair between the edge of the stripping blade and your thumb. Quickly pull the comb through the hair, and remove any loose hair caught inside the blade. Repeat the process along the dog's neck and back, and stop at the end of the tail. To minimize discomfort, pluck a few hairs at a time.

Once you have finished stripping your dog, spray his coat with a light coat conditioner. This gives the coat moisture, and soothes skin that has been irritated by stripping. Distribute the conditioner evenly by rubbing your hands over the coat.

CHAPTER 10

Cairn Terrier Exercise: How Can You Keep Your Cairn Terrier Fit?

C airn Terriers are smart dogs, they need both physical and mental stimulation in order to remain healthy. If you don't allow your dog to exercise, he will become disobedient, destructive, and will put on weight.

It is important that you take weather into consideration when exercising your Cairn. Weather that is too hot, or too cold, can be dangerous. During these times, allow your dog to exercise inside, you can play some of the games under the mental exercise section in the home. The key is to keep your dog active for a minimum of one hour.

Cairn Terriers and Physical Exercise

The most common physical exercises are runs, walks, and games of fetch. If you can't fit a full hour into your schedule, break it up so that you do 30 minutes in the morning, and 30 minutes in the evening.

Before taking your Cairn for a run, he needs to know that you set the pace, you don't want him running off ahead of you.

Fetch: Fetch requires both physical and mental agility, it is a fun game that both you and your Cairn will enjoy.

1. Hold your dog's favorite toy in your hand and show it to him. Throw the toy a short distance.
2. Praise him as he chases the toy.
3. When he picks up the toy and starts bringing it back to you, praise him.
4. If he doesn't bring the toy back to you, don't chase him, but encourage him to bring the toy back to you.
5. When he gets to you, catch the toy, by placing your left hand underneath his mouth.
6. Say "Drop it," or "Give," and then use your right hand to put a treat close to his nose.
7. When he lets go of the toy, give him the treat and praise him.
8. You can start this game in the hallway, once your Cairn understands the game, you can start playing it outside.

Chase: Cairn Terriers were born to chase and catch their prey which is why your puppy will love this game.

1. Tie one of his favorite toys to the end of a strong piece of rope.
2. Attach the end that you will hold to a stick.
3. Drag the rope with the toy on it across the ground, or swing it around in the air a short distance off the ground, and let your dog chase it.
4. When he catches the toy, praise him.

Urban Agility: Dogs enjoy going for walks, but after a while, your Cairn will get bored of the routine. Incorporate some urban agility into your stroll to make it more exciting for both you and him. You won't need any special equipment for the game, just a creative eye; here are some ideas you might want to include:

- Putting his paws over the top of a fence or fire hydrant.
- Jumping from one surface to another (like a raised curb or a bench).
- Jumping onto a bench and sitting down.
- As you walk, allow your Cairn to weave in and out of your legs.

Add Some Weight: If you have ever gone hiking with a backpack, you know how tiring it can be. Adding some weight into a small doggy backpack is a great way to burn additional energy on a walk.

Cairn Terriers and Mental Exercise

Your Cairn Terrier will quickly get bored and start acting up if it goes through the same routine every day. Cairns are an intelligent breed, and they need to be stimulated and challenged mentally. Here are some creative ways to engage his brain:

The training process is mentally challenging for your dog, since Cairn Terriers learn quickly, you will need to search for new and more difficult tricks for him to work on. Here are some tricks you might want to consider:

Interactive Toys and Games: Challenge your pup with canine puzzles, or doggie board games. Dog dominoes and dog memory games, are especially fun. You can also purchase toys that let you hide treats and toys on the inside, he will then need to figure out how to retrieve the treat.

Ring Stackers: These toys teach puppies eye-mouth or eye-paw coordination. Ring stackers is a difficult game that will take days, or even weeks, to learn. Make sure you use wooden rings with natural dyes for this game, because he will spend a lot of time biting down on them. Because Cairn Terriers are small dogs, purchase smaller rings.

Clicker training is perfect for the ring stacker game, because your dog is feeling, instead of looking at what he is doing. Give your dog a treat when he picks up a ring, and as he moves the ring closer to the stick, click and treat him again. Continue shaping him by clicking and treating him, as he attempts to maneuver the ring over the stick.

You can make the game more challenging by mounting the stick against a wall, so that your dog will have to fit it onto a horizontal stick, instead of dropping it onto a vertical stick. You can also put the rings in another room so that your Cairn is running between rooms to collect and stack them, before getting the main prize.

New Trick: This activity enhances your dog's creativity, it is a well-loved game in clicker training, because it trains dogs to think independently and think about the type of behavior most likely to earn him a reward.

The main idea of the game is a simple one; any new behavior that your dog offers, click and treat him for it. If he displays behavior that has already been demonstrated, ignore it.

A typical game will involve you saying, "new trick," your dog will perform an action such as to sit or lie down. Click and treat then say "new trick" again, he will then do something like stand up and run around in a circle. After saying "new trick" and he offers the same behavior, say, "you have already done that," and don't give him a reward. Then say "new trick" again and see what he comes up with. This game can last 30 to 40 minutes at a time.

If your Cairn is not used to clicker training to shape behavior, make the game easier by rewarding him for the smallest action. For example, place a box next to your dog and click and treat him if he touches the box with his paw, walks around it, steps into it, or looks at the box. Basically, reward him for the slightest interaction with the box. The main idea of the game is still the same, so don't reward your Cairn if he repeats the same action twice. Once your dog becomes familiar with the game, expand it to other behaviors such as sit up, crawl, sit down, and so on. He will soon start creating his own behaviors to get a treat.

52-Toy Pick Up: This game will encourage your Cairn to clean up after himself. Start by putting a toy in your dog's mouth and then commanding him to "drop it." Getting your pup to drop a toy on command is the most important component of the game. He will then be able to progress to the next stage of the game, which is dropping the toy in a particular location. Once he has mastered the "drop it" command, start training him to drop toys into a box or basket. Click and treat each stage of his behavior such as your dog walking with the toy in his mouth in the direction of the basket, or leaving the toy next to the basket. With some practice, your dog will learn that a command such as "put it away" will mean pick up the toy, drop it into the basket and leave it there.

Once he has mastered this part of the game, make it more challenging by increasing the number of toys your Cairn picks up. Start by treating him each time he drops a toy into the basket, and then only reward him when he drops two toys into the basket, and then three, etc. Eventually, you should only reward him when he has dropped all toys into the basket.

It will take a while for your dog to master this game, so have some patience, and enjoy the journey with him.

Hot and Cold: This is an ideal game for clicker training because it follows the basic rules for shaping new behavior. The nature of this game might lead your Cairn to get a bit frustrated, but he will start to enjoy it once he gets the hang of it.

For the owner, the game is simple; all you need to do is sit on a chair with a bag of treats saying "hot" or "cold" the closer or further away he gets from what you have told him to do. For example, you might notice that your keys are on the floor and ask your dog to pick them up and deliver them to you. After you have given him the command, each time he moves closer to the keys, say "hot" with excitement in your voice and throw a treat in the direction of the keys. If your dog moves in the opposite direction of the keys, say "cold" in a quiet voice, and don't throw him a treat, so he knows he is not moving in the right direction. When he starts moving towards the direction of the keys, say "hot" again in an excited voice and throw him a treat. Keep doing this, until he picks up the keys and brings them to you.

There is plenty of room for creativity in this game, and you can get him to perform any behavior you can think of, such as getting a blanket from the couch, getting in and out of his crate, etc.

The Name Game: The name game teaches your dog to put toys away by name. You start by teaching him the name of the toy and then telling him to go and fetch it. Repetition is the most important aspect of this game because this is how he will learn the name of each toy.

You can start by holding up a toy, saying the name, allowing your dog to grab it, and then rewarding him for grabbing it. Let's say it's a dog chew toy called "Chewy," hold Chewy in one hand and say "Chewy," let your dog grab Chewy, and give him a reward. Repeat this between 20 and 30 times, until he understands. Then place Chewy next to a different toy such as a ball called Circle. Say "Chewy" to your dog, and see which toy he picks up. If he picks up Circle instead of Chewy, don't say anything, instead, place Chewy back next to Circle and say "Chewy" again. Once your dog starts picking up Chewy consistently, start again by placing Chewy next to a different toy, and keep repeating the process, until he is continuously choosing Chewy over the other toy.

Once your Cairn has learned the name of one toy, start the game again with a different toy. But don't place the other toy next to Chewy, choose a toy that you have not yet taught him the name of.

Once your dog has learned the names of two toys, for example Chewy and Circle, place the toys next to each other, and call out one name at a time, to see which one he picks up. Keep calling out the name "Chewy," until he is consistently picking up Chewy, and then move onto Circle.

Once he has mastered this, increase the intensity of the game by placing Chewy and Circle amongst a group of toys he does not know the names of, and then command him to fetch Chewy and Circle out of the group.

You can choose to teach your Cairn to learn as many names as you wish.

Shell Game: The shell game is simple but challenging. Take two opaque plastic cups and turn them over. Let your dog watch you put a treat under one of the cups. Indicate to your dog that you want him to come, and turn over the cup to get the treat. If your Cairn chooses the right cup, give him the treat, if he chooses the wrong cup, don't give him the treat but lift the cup up with the treat underneath it and show him. Keep repeating this, until your dog has figured out the trick. Even though Cairn Terriers are intelligent dogs, they will find it hard to understand how the treat keeps switching cups, but they will learn to understand it with practice.

Once your dog has learned how to play the game, increase the intensity, by randomly swapping sides. See if he can use his nose, eyes and thinking skills to locate the treat, after it has been switched over. This is a difficult game, and very few dogs master this stage, so don't jump to the conclusion that your Cairn might have a learning difficulty, if he doesn't get it.

Hide and Seek: You will need at least two people to play this game. One person will tell your dog to sit and stay, while the other person hides. Once they are well hidden, give the command for your Cairn to start looking, when he finds the person, give him a treat.

Treasure Hunt: Getting your dog to hunt down hidden treasure with his sense of smell is an effective brain stimulation method, it also teaches him how to use his senses. This is a difficult game, so you will want to make it simple at first, so that your dog doesn't get upset and give up.

You can start by giving him the sit-stay command, let him watch you hide one of his favorite toys or treats, then release him to go and find it. Give him a massive reward for finding it.

Once your Cairn understands the rules of the game, make it a little bit harder for him. Hide the toy or treat in another room or in a location where the smell of the treat or toy is masked, such as under the food dish or at the bottom of the laundry basket.

You can make the game really challenging by using cardboard boxes. Set up between 10-20 different sized cardboard boxes and put the reward underneath one of the boxes without him seeing. Let your dog examine the boxes, until he finds the treat and give him a reward when he finds it.

Jump Rope: This game teaches your Cairn to use body and eye coordination. Your dog must focus on the pace of the rope, when it hits a certain spot on the ground as well as jumping! Sounds impossible but if any dog can play this game successfully, a Cairn Terrier can!

Start by teaching your dog to focus on an object on the ground, such as a stick. Once he is focused on the stick, teach him to jump on that spot when you tell him to. Once he has learned how to do this, add the rope, and tell your dog to jump each time the rope comes down. This game will take a lot of patience and energy; but stick to it, once he learns how to play properly, he will start having fun.

CHAPTER 11

Cairn Terrier Health Issues: How Can I Reduce Their Likelihood?

T he Cairn Terrier is generally a fit and healthy dog; however, they do have some hereditary health issues that all potential owners should be aware of.

The more you know about potential health problems, the better you can prepare for them.

Cairn Terrier Health Problems – What Type of Health Problems Should I Look Out For? And How Can I Try To Prevent Them?

Cairn Terrier Hip Problems: Hip dysplasia and legg-calve-perthes are the most common hip problems, experienced by Cairn Terriers.

Hip Dysplasia: Hip dysplasia is characterized by an under-developed and shallow acetabulum (the socket part of the joint). This deformity causes harsh friction in the area when it moves. The muscles develop slowly, making weight-bearing difficult, and so the joint becomes unstable and loose. This causes accelerated wear and tear, which then leads to inflammation, and additional pain.

Hip dysplasia is a genetic disease triggered by a polygenic trait. This means that several pairs of genes play a role in the condition.

Symptoms: During the beginning stages of the condition, there may not be any symptoms. However, as it develops, you will notice that your dog will start finding it difficult to walk. To relieve the pain, dogs tend to walk on both of their hind legs at the same time, making it appear that they are impersonating a bunny.

The hind legs may also start to wobble, or he might start limping because one leg is more painful than the other. Inflammation and pain become a part of the problem later. You may find that your dog is stiff when he wakes up in the morning and will not want to stand up, jump or climb the stairs.

You will know that your dog is in pain if he displays any of the following:

- Has an unusual gait
- Finds it difficult to climb the stairs
- Finds it difficult to get up and lie down
- Becomes less active

Diagnosis: An X-ray will determine whether your dog is suffering from hip dysplasia. However, it cannot determine the level of pain he is in. To get a good quality X-ray, your vet may suggest that he is sedated. The vet will also look at how your Cairn moves and walks, because conditions such as elbow dysplasia, cruciate ligament tears, and lower back problems, can cause similar symptoms.

Treatment: There is no cure for hip dysplasia, medication will make your dog more comfortable, but it is a condition that he will have to live with for the rest of his life. The aim of the treatment is to ensure that he is not in continuous pain and has a good quality of life.

Your vet will recommend that his activities are restricted and to relieve pain and inflammation prescribe him with a non-steroidal anti-inflammatory. He should always be kept on a leash, and forbidden from running, jumping, or any form of hard playing. If your Cairn likes water, swimming is a great way to relax the muscles and relieve pain. It is also easier to walk your dog on soft surfaces, such as unpaved grassy areas.

You can make your pet more comfortable by buying him a pressure-reducing bed, ramp, and stairs.

Physical therapy such as hydrotherapy, massage, and underwater treadmills, can help to reduce the pain and swelling.

There is a possibility that your dog might need surgery, this is often performed as a preventative measure to halt the onset of degenerative joint disease. In general, dogs who don't get any relief from medication, will have surgery. Surgical procedures could include a hip replacement or reshaping the joint.

Prevention: Prevention is always going to be better than cure, so if your puppy is susceptible to hip dysplasia, make sure that he doesn't put on any excess weight, and reduce strenuous activities, so that he doesn't put any unnecessary stress on his hips.

If your dog is overweight, you should put him on a strict low-calorie diet. Your vet may also give him a Glucosamine supplement to help with joint repair.

There is no genetic testing for the condition, and there are also additional behaviors that exacerbate the condition.

Exercise: Puppies grow at an accelerated rate, during this stage, your dog can develop hip dysplasia, especially if he is a puppy who enjoys jumping to catch a ball or a frisbee. Puppies will start showing signs of hip dysplasia between four and 12 months of age.

Diet: If your puppy is susceptible to the condition, a high-calorie diet can increase his risk of developing the disease. Increased weight gain can lead to obesity, which puts a lot of strain on the hips. Additionally, diets that do not contain enough phosphorous and calcium have a negative effect on bone development.

Legg-Calve-Perthes: Legg-Calve-Perthes disease is the deterioration of the bones in the hind legs. This leads to joint inflammation and decaying of the hip joint.

Causes: The exact cause of the condition has yet to be determined; however, one of the common traits among dogs who suffer from the disease is an issue with blood supply to the bones.

Symptoms: Your dog may be suffering from legg-calve-perthes, if he displays any of the following symptoms:

• Pain when the hip joint is moved
• Thigh muscle wastage, in the affected limb
• Carrying the affected limb
• Lameness

Diagnosis: You will need to provide your vet with your dog's full medical history. This should include how long he has had the symptoms for. The dog is given a thorough physical examination and an X-ray is taken. When the disease is in its early stages, the X-ray will show decreased bone density, widening of joint space, and thickening of the femoral bone neck. As the disease progresses, the affected area will show new bone growth, extreme deformation of the femoral head, and a possible femoral neck fracture.

Treatment: If the disease is in the beginning stages, your vet will prescribe medication for pain management. It is also important that your dog is kept on a strict diet to prevent weight gain.

In severe cases where the dog is not responding to medical treatment, there is a high chance that your Cairn will need to have surgery. The most common surgery performed for this condition, is a femoral head and neck osteotomy (FHO).

Another operation he could have is a total hip replacement (THR). Studies show that the results are similar between the FHO and the THR surgery; however, the FHO is the most common because it is not as expensive as the THR. If your dog does not respond to the FHO surgery, he will then have THR.

After surgery, your dog will require pain medication and physical therapy, to assist in the recovery process. It is also advised that your Cairn takes supplements for the long-term, such as glucosamine for cartilage protection.

It is also important to note that dogs suffering from legg-calve-perthes should not be used for breeding.

Cairn Terrier Allergies

Cairn Terriers can develop allergies to anything from dust to food. They can start at any time during your dog's life. There are four types of allergies your Cairn Terrier can be exposed to:

- Atopy (airborne)
- Food
- Flea
- Contact

Atopy: Atopy is also referred to as "atopic dermatitis," It is a common condition where allergens in the environment cause an allergic reaction on the skin. Common allergens include:

- Mold spores
- House dust mites
- Pollen from trees, grass, and weeds

Food: Dogs with food allergies are usually allergic to proteins that come from animal or plant-based ingredients. When dogs ingest proteins, they are broken down into molecules that the immune system mistakes as a threat.

Flea: Fleabites are going to make any dog itch, but some Cairn Terriers are allergic to pests. You will hear your vet refer to a flea allergy as fleabite hypersensitivity, or flea allergy dermatitis (FAD). FAD is the most common skin disease in America; flea allergies are worse during the summer, if your dog suffers from seasonal allergies, he is more likely to have an allergic reaction to fleabites.

Contact: When a Cairn Terrier gets an allergic reaction to something he has encountered, his body will react to a certain type of molecule called an allergen. These allergens can come from:

- Weed pollens
- Grass
- Trees
- Fabrics, such as nylon or wool
- Food ingredients such as soy, grains, or meats

- Plastic and rubber materials
- Dust mites and house dust
- Flea bites

When these allergens are ingested, inhaled, or come into contact with a dog's body, the immune system produces a protein called IgE. They attach themselves to tissue mast cells in the skin, which stimulate the release of certain types of chemicals, such as histamines. It is this that causes the skin to itch.

If your cairn terrier is displaying one or more of the following symptoms, there is a high chance he is suffering from allergies:

- Diarrhea
- Vomiting
- Bumps, lumps, rashes
- Sneezing and wheezing
- Coughing
- Itchy ears
- Ear infection
- Red eyes
- Watery eyes
- Swollen, red paws
- Excessive chewing and licking of the feet
- Runny nose
- Rubbing head against furniture

Treatment: Unfortunately, there are no cures for allergies; to limit and reduce irritation, the best course of action is preventative measures.

Contact Allergies: If your dog is allergic to certain items he comes into contact with, remove the items that trigger a reaction from his environment.

Food Allergies: Hypoallergenic dog food is designed for dogs who are allergic to normal dog food. There should be no artificial preservatives, flavors or colors in hypoallergenic foods. Before changing your Cairn Terrier's diet, consult your vet for advice. Although he is allergic to the food he is currently eating, a sudden change in diet may make his condition worse.

Once your vet has given you the all-clear, start feeding your dog according to the manufacturer's instructions.

Finally, be patient, you might not notice results right away, but this doesn't mean it isn't working. Wait for a while and keep an eye out for positive changes in his behavior.

Flea Allergies: Your vet will recommend a topical, injection or oral flea treatment, but medication is only half the battle. Fleas live in bedding, carpets, and other surfaces in the home. Wash your bedding and throws often; also, vacuum your carpets, rugs and sofa cushions. Empty the vacuum bag outside to prevent the fleas from coming back into the house. You can also use flea spray on your carpets and furniture, but make sure you keep your family members away from the sprayed areas until they are dry.

To ease the irritation, you can give your dog a bath in cool water. Avoid using flea shampoos or other products, until you have taken your dog to the vet. Some of them contain harsh chemicals that can make his condition worse.

Finally, keep in contact with your vet, to make sure that the treatment plan provided is working, and to keep an eye out for any additional flea-related problems.

Atopy: Atopy dog allergies are typically seasonal, which makes them difficult to treat. A dust mite allergy will be worse during the winter, and a pollen allergy will be worse during the summer. This can give dog owners the impression that it is just a short-term phase. A vet will treat an atopy allergy, in one of the following ways:

- **Cyclosporine:** Cyclosporine is administered once a day for four weeks, and then reduced to every other day, or twice a week. It is an expensive treatment, and can have some undesirable side effects, such as diarrhea or stomach ache.
- **Steroids:** Steroids such as dexamethasone or prednisone are administered orally, by injection, or as a shampoo or topical ointment. Steroids are used as a short-term solution because they can lead to additional health risks such as diabetes, adrenal gland problems, and liver problems.
- **Immunosuppressive therapy:** Your Cairn Terrier might not respond to other treatments, and so will need a more intensive drug treatment, such as immunosuppressive therapy.
- **Topical treatments:** Topical treatments include ointments, leave-in conditioners, and medicated shampoos. Follow the instructions provided by your vet, and repeat often for the best results.

- **Fatty acid supplements:** They help to reduce skin inflammation and may be combined with additional medications.
- **Antihistamines**
- **Symptomatic therapy**

Cairn Terrier Skin Problems

There are several reasons why your dog might develop a skin condition. You will need to take him to the vet, for them to diagnose the underlying cause. In severe cases, your vet might recommend blood or skin tests, to help pinpoint the exact cause of the condition.

If the cause is related to a food source, your Cairn might also show symptoms of stomach upset. Typically, this will involve locating the exact ingredient that is causing the problem and eliminating it from his diet. If an allergen is the cause, your dog will be put on an elimination diet to isolate the allergen. Here are some common skin problems that your Cairn Terrier could experience:

Ringworm: Ringworm is an infection caused by fungus on the skin. Despite the name, there are no worms involved in this condition, as mentioned, it is a fungus that spreads around the skin.

Causes: Ringworm lives in soil, and since Cairn Terriers like to dig, they are more likely to catch the condition. They can also get exposed to ringworm through another infected animal, toys, bedding, brushes, or saddles.

Symptoms: If your dog is experiencing the following symptoms, there is a high chance that he could have ringworm.

Scaly skin

Patchy areas of hair loss

Lesions on the ears, paws, head, and limbs

In mild cases, there may not be any symptoms; whereas severe cases can result in scabby, inflamed lesions all over the skin.

Allergic Dermatitis: Allergic dermatitis is a skin condition resulting from your dog being allergic to food, or something in the environment.

Causes: An allergy is the most common cause of allergic dermatitis.

Symptoms: If your Cairn Terrier is experiencing the following symptoms, there is a high chance that he could have allergic dermatitis:

- Red bumps on the skin
- Scaly areas on the skin
- Thickened skin
- Darkened skin
- Bald spots
- Stained fur, due to continuous licking
- Shaking the head
- A foul smell on the skin

Yeast Infection: A yeast infection is a bacterial overgrowth that takes over an area of the body.

Causes: There are several factors that can contribute to a yeast infection; these include:

- Allergies
- Hormonal-disorders
- Prolonged use of steroids or antibiotics
- Cancer
- External skin parasites
- Immune system suppressive drugs

Symptoms: If your Cairn Terrier is experiencing the following symptoms, there is a high chance that he could have a yeast infection.

- Extreme itching
- Greasy coat
- Sores on the skin
- Hearing loss
- Foul-smelling skin
- Skin irritation
- Skin inflammation
- Red skin
- Hair loss

Treatment: Your vet will recommend a range of treatments to help treat and manage your dog's skin problems. These include:

- Therapeutic diets
- Medical treatments
- Food supplements
- Pet shampoos

Diet plays an important role in eliminating skin conditions in dogs. Diets that are high in omega-3 fatty acids, can get rid of the itching associated with allergic dermatitis.

In most cases, skin conditions are resolved quickly with a dose of medication, it is rare that your Cairn will need long-term treatment for a skin condition.

Cairn Terrier Hypoallergenic – Are Cairn Terriers Hypoallergenic?

A hypoallergic dog is one that is more compatible with those who suffer from allergies. Cairn terriers have got dense coats, which means they don't shed much. They also don't have as much dander as other dogs.

Cairn Terrier Eye Problems

Healthy eyes in your Cairn Terrier are essential to a good quality of life. Unfortunately, there are eye conditions that affect some dogs more than others, it is important that pet owners are able to recognize symptoms so that they can get their dog the help he needs, as soon as possible. Here are some of the most common eye problems in Cairn Terriers.

Cataracts: Your dog's eye is covered by a transparent lens, beams of light are focused onto the retina through the lens, enabling your dog to see. A cataract occurs when the lens fibers are disrupted, causing a partial or full blocking of the lens. A small cataract is not as problematic as a large one, which could lead to complete blindness.

Causes: Cataracts are due to old age, or they can be hereditary. However, genetics are the most common cause. They can be present when your dog is firstborn, or develop as he grows. The following conditions will also cause cataracts to develop:

- Diabetes
- Cancer therapy treatment
- Toxic substance exposure
- Birth defects
- Eye injuries or trauma
- Nutritional deficiencies or disorders
- Eye inflammation
- Eye infection

Pet owners often mistake a condition called nuclear sclerosis for a cataract. It causes your dog's eyes to turn gray, and appears in dogs at the age of five. However, the condition rarely interferes with vision, and neither does it require treatment.

Symptoms: If your dog develops cataracts you will notice the following symptoms:

- A bluish, white, or gray layer in the eye
- Clumsiness
- Scratching or rubbing of the eyes
- Afraid to climb the stairs or jump up onto furniture
- Excessive blinking
- Eye irritation
- Redness of the eye

Diagnosis: Your vet will perform a complete physical examination on your dog; this will include a series of eye tests. Depending on the specific needs of your Cairn Terrier, your vet may suggest that you take him to see a specialist eye doctor called a veterinary ophthalmologist. They will perform different tests, to determine the underlying cause of the condition. These might include:

- Polymerase chain reaction and culture testing, to analyze how the retina is working
- A complete blood count
- Chemistry tests to check for liver, pancreatic and kidney diseases and sugar levels

Treatment: The most effective treatment for cataracts is surgery. However, this will depend on the severity of the cataract. Although they will not cause your dog any pain, he is at risk of going blind. Surgery will correct his vision by removing the damaged lens, and replacing it with an acrylic or plastic prosthetic lens, to provide focused vision. There is a 90 to 95 percent success rate for this surgery.

Your vet might prescribe your dog with oral supplements. They act as antioxidants, and help to reduce inflammation in the eyes.

Until his eyes heal, your Cairn will need to wear a protective collar (Elizabethan Collar). You will also need to reduce his activity levels, and keep him calm and quiet. He will require several eye drops per day, for a few weeks after the surgery.

Progressive Retinal Atrophy (PRA): Progressive Retinal Atrophy is a disorder in dogs that affects the rod cells, and damages the retina. The end result of the disease is blindness in both eyes.

Causes: It has been determined that the disease is hereditary caused by an autosomal recessive gene, carried by both parents. Even if the parents do not suffer from the condition, they can produce puppies who do.

Symptoms: If your Cairn is displaying the following symptoms, he might be suffering from PRA:

- A green tint to the eye
- Gray discoloration to the eye
- Reduced vision at night time
- Afraid to jump off furniture at night
- Scared to walk up or down stairs
- Stumbling or tripping over objects
- Bumping into walls or furniture

- Pupils are slow to respond to light
- Fisting the air when walking down the stairs

Diagnosis: Progressive Retinal Atrophy is diagnosed through a series of eye examinations by a veterinary ophthalmologist.

Treatment: At present, there is no known treatment for the condition. Some vets recommend prolonging the dog's vision, and slowing down the progression of the disease, with antioxidant therapy.

Lens Luxation: Lens luxation is a dislocation of the lens, it moves either to the front or the back of the eye.

Causes: The main cause of the condition is hereditary, but it is also caused by a weakening of the threads that hold the lens in place, eye inflammation, glaucoma, and cataracts.

Symptoms: If your dog is displaying any of the following symptoms, he may be suffering from lens luxation.

- Red eyes
- Sore eyes
- Depression
- Reluctant to go for walks
- A bluish tint over the cornea

Diagnosis: Your vet will give your dog a complete physical examination, and then refer him to a veterinary ophthalmologist. It is not a difficult condition to diagnose, because once the lens has been dislocated, it is easy to see that it is out of position.

Treatment: In the worst cases of lens luxation, surgery is required to remove the entire eye. However, when the condition is in its primary stages, medicinal treatment is provided.

Cairn Terrier Life Expectancy – Cairn Terrier Old Age – How Long Will My Dog Live?

The average life span of the cairn terrier is between 12-15 years. Cairn terriers who die early typically do so because of hereditary health complications. But like humans, if you want your dog to live out its full years, a proper diet and the right amount of exercise are essential.

When Cairn Terriers start aging, they need a lot of special care and attention. As they enter into their golden years, there is an increased risk of health complications. You will notice subtle physical differences when your Cairn Terrier starts aging such as:

- A graying muzzle
- Reduced muscle tone
- His coat will get coarser
- He will either gain weight or lose it
- They find it harder to regulate their body temperature
- Their strength and stamina diminish
- His immune system will start to break down, so he is more likely to catch infections
- He may develop arthritis
- His mental capacity will start to decrease, so he won't be as quick to respond

- His vision and hearing will become impaired, so he will find it difficult to respond to external stimuli
- He will start getting fussy with his food
- He won't like change
- Pain will affect him more
- He might start feeling disorientated

As your Cairn Terrier grows older, you will need to take on more responsibilities. This includes keeping an eye on his dental health, how often his bed needs changing, and his diet and the amount of exercise he gets. His dietary needs will change as he gets older, he will need a better quality of food and you will also need to pay attention to his weight. The following feeding guide will give you an idea of the food he needs; but you should bear in mind that the food should be easy to digest, and free from additives:

- Fat: Below 10 percent
- Protein: Between 14-21 percent
- Sodium: Between 0.2-0.4 percent
- Calcium: Between 0.5-0.8 percent
- Fiber: Below 4 percent
- Phosphorous: Between 0.4-0.7 percent

Your older Cairn Terrier will still need exercise, but not as much as when he was younger. Continuous exercise will prevent him from losing muscle tone and gaining weight. He will also need easier access to fresh, clean water, because as they age, Cairn Terriers are more at risk of developing kidney disorders.

CHAPTER 12

Cairn Terrier Breeding: Should Your Breed Your Cairn Terrier?

I f you are thinking about breeding your Cairn Terrier, there are certain things you will need to think about. Here are some questions you should ask yourself before going ahead.

There are a lot of things you will need to consider before breeding your Cairn Terrier.

Should I Breed My Cairn Terrier? What Should I Consider?

- Is the female dog fit and healthy enough to breed?
- Does the female dog have a good temperament?
- Am I financially secure enough to pay for the required health tests, for the female dog and her litter when they are born?
- Do I understand the whelping process?
- Will I be able to afford to pay for a caesarean section, if required?
- Will I be able to handle a litter of 10 or 12 puppies?
- Do I have enough knowledge to rear the litter?
- Do I have the time to dedicate to the litter, until they find their own homes?
- Will I be able to find loving and decent homes for the puppies?
- Will I be able to rehome any of the puppies, if things don't work out with the owners?

If you can't answer yes to all these questions, you might want to reconsider breeding. If you decide against it, then you should start looking into getting her spayed, to prevent unwanted pregnancy.

Cairn Terrier Breeding – Checklist For a Novice Breeder

If you have decided to go ahead and breed your Cairn Terrier, you will need to consider the following:

- Responsible breeders are of the mindset that each litter they produce should be better than the parents.

- Responsible breeders take seriously, soundness, temperament and health.
- Responsible breeders are forward-thinking and have a plan for each mating session, to make sure that their puppies are bred in the best possible environment.
- Responsible breeders accept full responsibility for the puppies they have bred.

What Do I Do Before Breeding My Cairn Terrier?

- Make sure the dog is licensed.
- Depending on your country, make sure your dog is microchipped.
- Get a DNA profile for your dog.
- Get a Kennel Name.
- Check that there have been no breeding endorsements attached to your dog's records.
- Make sure that your dog is healthy enough, both physically and mentally, to whelp a litter.
- Have your dog thoroughly examined e.g.: DNA testing, eye testing, elbow grading, and hip scoring.
- Contact a breed society, to get more information about the breed.
- Make sure that the male dog is healthy.
- Contact the breeder of your female dog, as they might be able to give you additional information.

What Do I Do If I Want To Breed My Cairn Terrier as a Stud?

Mating Cairn Terriers for the first time is a difficult process. If you plan to use your male dog as a stud, you will need to start preparing him from a young age. Here are some tips for breeding your male.

Female Dog's Season

The best time to pair your dog with a female, is when she is in season, this is also referred to as "heat." During this time, she will experience the following:

- On the first day, she will start bleeding.
- For one week, she will not be able to stand the company of a male dog during this time. She will do everything in her power to get away from your male dog, including snapping at him and running away. However, this is the best time for flirting and getting to know each other, so it is important that they are paired together.
- There will be a week during her heat cycle where she will want the attention of any stud, and will go out of her way to find one.
- She will then go through another week where she runs from the advances of a stud.

Male Dogs and Mating

The best days to for dogs to get together and mate are day 9, 11 and 13, and again on day 10, 12 and 14. You will need at least three people to ensure that the stud does not pull out too early.

- Let the dogs flirt and play around with each other
- If the female is taller than the male, you will either need to make a hollow for the female or prop the male up.
- Allow the male dog to enter her.
- Make sure the male stays in and doesn't slip out, or the sperm will end up on the floor.

Tie: The ideal circumstance is that male and female tie together. Position the dogs so their backs are together. Don't allow them to start roaming around, if you get a tie, you will still need to mate them a couple of days later. A female dog can get pregnant after one tie, but it is better to get two or three.

Cairn Terrier Whelping – What Should I Do Before The Whelping?

It is important to ensure that your female dog is relaxed and comfortable prior to whelping; therefore, you will need to make certain preparations to ensure that she is able to adjust to any changes in her environment and food before the birth. Set aside a comfortable area where she feels at home for whelping and raising puppies. The puppies should remain safe, warm and confined, but the mother should be able to come and go as she pleases.

It is essential that you are properly prepared for the birth of puppies, so here is a checklist to ensure that you have everything in order.

- Feed the female dog premium quality adult dog food until she is four weeks pregnant. You will then need to make a gradual switch to puppy food. By her final week of pregnancy, she should be consuming all puppy food.

- Approximately two weeks before your female dog gives birth, provide her with a whelping box to give birth in. The box should be big enough for both the litter and the mother to stretch out in. The female dog should be able to come and go without any difficulty. The sides of the box should be several inches high so that the puppies can't get out and draughts can't come in. Leave the whelping box in a quiet, warm area where there are no distractions. Cover the bottom of the box with puppy training pads or newspaper, you can also use towels, rugs and blankets, and then layer it with plastic sheets. For an additional heat source, you can place a waterproof heating pad under the box.

- Once the puppies can move around, make sure they have a safe and confined area to play in. Make sure you use puppy training pads.

- If there are any problems prior to your female dog giving birth, you may need to hand feed the puppies with a commercial milk replacement formula. Use a syringe to feed the puppies when required.

- Make sure you have the contact details for your vet and emergency number to hand, in case there are any complications. If your dog spends more than half an hour actively straining without giving birth, you will need to call the vet.

What Do I Do After Breeding My Cairn Terrier?

Once your female dog has given birth to her litter, you will need to take care of them for approximately eight weeks until you can start finding them homes. It is important that you find dog owners who will love the puppies just as much as you and that they will be happy in their new environment.

When making the decision about who to sell to, you should consider the following:

- Find out how much the potential buyers know about Cairn Terriers.
- Arrange to meet the entire family, including children, if they have any.
- Ask them if they have any other pets.
- Find out the buyers' intentions for the dog, do they want to breed at a later date, or do they want the puppy solely as a pet.
- Advertise on your Kennel Club's site.
- Be open and honest about the characteristics of the dog. If he has got behavioral problems, let them know.
- Ask how long they spend out of the home going to work etc. Will they be able to take the dog with them?
- Find out about their living conditions, do they have a garden with a fence? You might want to go to the house to ensure that the location is satisfactory.
- If you do not feel as if the buyers are the right fit for the puppy, don't sell it.

CHAPTER 13

What Do You Do In An Emergency?

E very year dogs in the United States are involved in road traffic accidents, swallow poisonous substances, or suffer from heatstroke. Knowing what to do if one of these situations were to occur could save your dog's life.

Knowing what to do in an emergency situation, could save your dog's life.

What To Have In Your First Aid Kit

You should always make sure that you have the following equipment in your first aid kit:

- Surgical sticky tape
- A roll of crepe or self-adhesive bandages (5cm width)
- A box of cotton balls
- A box of absorbent sterile gauze
- A blunt curved scissors
- An Elizabethan collar
- Dressings to bind open wounds (non-adhesive absorbent) 5x5cm
- A thick towel

Cairn Terrier Emergencies – How To Handle an Emergency

Here are the steps you would need to take, if there was an emergency with your Cairn Terrier:

- Ensure that you and others are safe. Remain calm and pay attention to your surroundings before doing anything. Injured dogs are in pain and frightened, regardless of whether you are his owner, he might bite you if he is touched.
- Call your vet; always make sure you have their contact information which should include their name, phone number and address. There might not be a vet available, but other staff members will be able to give you instructions.

- Before calling, make sure you have a pen available, just in case you are given another number to call.

- It is always better to take your dog to the vet's location instead of waiting for them to come out to you.

- Put a muzzle on your dog if there is a risk of biting. If you don't have a muzzle, wrap tape around his nose and behind his ears. Don't do this if he is finding it difficult to breathe. You can also restrain your Cairn, by placing a thick towel over his head.

- Do not give human pain medication to your dog, it will cause more damage. He may need an anesthetic, so don't feed him, or give him a drink.

- Although you will feel the need to rush, drive carefully when taking your dog to the vet.

- If your dog does bite you, go and see your doctor immediately.

Does Your Cairn Terrier Need Emergency Assistance?

If you are concerned about your dog outside of normal hours, you can call your vet for advice. You should contact your vet if:

- Your dog does not want to get up, feels weak, or is depressed

- Your dog is unable to use the toilet. Blockage of the bladder is common in males, and can be fatal if left untreated

- Your dog has difficulty breathing, or his breathing is loud or fast

- Your dog can't stop coughing

- Your dog appears to be in a lot of pain

- Your dog can't stop vomiting

- Diarrhea mixed with blood

- Your dog is unable to balance properly
- A female dog with suckling puppies is shaking, shivering, agitated, and will not settle. She may have eclampsia, which is a serious condition needing urgent medical attention.

What To Do If Your Cairn Terrier Is In a Road Accident

Cairn Terriers are very energetic and hyperactive, as previously stated they are known to run out into the road, if they see something they like. Therefore, it is important to keep your dog on a leash, at all times. Make sure the collar is not loose, so that he can't get free.

In the unfortunate event that he does get run over, pay attention to the moving vehicles, speak gently to your dog to calm him down. Don't make any sudden movements, and if you do have to move, do so slowly. If you can, put a lead on him, and if necessary, muzzle him before touching him. If your dog is able to walk, take him to the vet, even if it doesn't seem like he is in any pain, go anyway because he might have internal injuries.

If your Cairn is unable to walk, pick him up by placing one hand on the front of his chest, and the other underneath his hindquarters. You should also cover him with a blanket so that he doesn't get cold.

What To Do If Your Cairn Terrier Is Bleeding

Keep your dog quiet and calm and wrap a tight bandage around the wound. If you don't have a bandage to hand, use a piece of clothing or a towel. If blood is leaking through, tightly apply another layer. You may need to use a tourniquet (a constricting or compressing device to stop blood flow), but that should be your last resort. If you are unable to bandage certain places, firmly press a pad onto the wound, and use your hand to hold it in place. Take your dog to the vet immediately.

If you have your first aid kit with you when the accident happens, use a non-adhesive swab or cotton bandage, and then put a layer of cotton wool over the top. Cover this with another cotton bandage and use surgical tape to stick it down. If you are bandaging limbs but the foot has not been injured, you will need to bandage it as well, so that it doesn't swell up.

What To Do If Your Cairn Terrier Gets Burned

Run cold water over the burn for a minimum of five minutes, and then call your vet. Do not apply any creams or ointments to the injury; however, if it is going to be a while before you get to the vet, soak a dressing in saline, and apply it to the area. Cover the dog with a blanket to keep him warm.

What To Do If Your Cairn Terrier Breaks a Bone

If your dog is bleeding, deal with that first. Do not apply a splint to the broken limb, as this will cause him additional pain, and it can cause the bone to come out through the skin. Put your Cairn in a crate and take him to the vet.

What To Do If Your Cairn Terrier Has Been Poisoned

Call the vet right away, at the same time as locating the packaging of the offending substance. If you suspect he has eaten a plant, try and find out the name. Do not force your dog to vomit, unless your vet instructs you to.

What To Do If Your Cairn Terrier Has a Ball Stuck In His Throat

Get to the vet as soon as possible. You can try and push the ball out by pressing on the throat.

If his tongue or gums start to turn blue, or your dog has collapsed, you will need to get someone to help you with the following procedure. One person will need to hold his mouth open, while the other puts their fingers into his mouth and attempts to retrieve the ball. If you can't get it out, turn the dog on his side while the other person is still holding his mouth open, and push down sharply, and suddenly onto the stomach just behind the rib cage. The other person should be ready to get the ball, when it comes out.

What To Do If Your Cairn Terrier Has a Swollen Stomach

Call the vet immediately, a swollen stomach might be a sign of a life-threatening condition. You will notice that your dog is dribbling, gulping, and trying to vomit.

What To Do If Your Cairn Terrier's Coat Becomes Contaminated

If a substance such as tar or paint spills onto your dog's coat or paws, make sure he doesn't lick it, or he could get poisoned. Use an Elizabethan collar, if you have one available. You might be able to snip off small areas of the affected hair. Never use paint remover or turpentine on your dog, as these substances can be equally as dangerous. You can give him a bath in washing liquid.

However, if the spillage was substantial, you will need to take your dog to the vet.

What To Do If Your Cairn Terrier Is Having a Seizure

Do not try and hold and comfort your dog if he is having a seizure. This will stimulate him and can cause the seizure to last longer. Instead, turn the lights down in the room and reduce any noise.

Remove all items away from the dog, especially electrical items. Pad the area where he is lying with cushions and call the vet.

What To Do If Your Cairn Terrier Has Heat Stroke

If it is a warm day, or he has been exercising and playing, and your dog feels distressed and starts panting heavily, he may be suffering from heatstroke. Take your dog out of the heat and put him into a cool area. Wet his coat with lukewarm water (do not use cold water, it slows heat loss by contracting the blood vessels in the skin). Give him a small amount of water to drink, and call the vet.

What To Do If Your Cairn Terrier Has Got An Eye Injury

If the eye is sticking out of the socket, place a wet dressing over it. Prevent the dog from scratching or rubbing and call the vet. If your dog managed to get chemicals in his eyes, if you have one to hand, use an eye drop bottle to rinse them with water, and call the vet.

What To Do If Your Cairn Terrier Gets Into a Fight

If your dog appears distressed, shocked, or dull after a fight, call the vet. Otherwise, inspect the wound. If he has got a puncture wound to the body or the head, call the vet immediately. Injuries to the limbs might not need immediate attention, unless they are very painful. But you should take your dog to the vet within 24 hours, because he might need antibiotics.

What To Do If Your Cairn Terrier Is Drowning

Don't try and rescue your dog alone, because you might put yourself at risk. If he does manage to get out of the water, wipe away any debris from his mouth and nose. Pick the dog up by his hind legs, and hold him in an upside-down position, until all the water has drained from his lungs. If he has stopped breathing, give him mouth to mouth resuscitation. Even if it looks like your dog has recovered, go and see the vet, because it is common for there to be complications after the event has occurred.

What To Do If Your Cairn Terrier Has Been Stung

Pull the stinger out below the poison sac, and rinse the area with water. If you have it available, use a mixture of bicarbonate soda and water. An ice pack will also help to soothe the pain from the sting. If the sting is in the throat or the mouth, take your dog to the vet, because it could have an effect on his breathing.

What To Do If Your Cairn Terrier Gets An Electric Shock

If the shock happens outside the home with a high voltage supply, do not go near the scene as you will put yourself at risk. Instead, call the police.

If the shock happens at home, cut off the power supply. If you are unable to do this, use a non-metallic dry item, such as a broom handle to push the dog away from the power source. If he has stopped breathing, you will need to perform resuscitation and call the vet straight away.

How To Perform Basic Resuscitation

- Lay the dog on his side
- Hold a wisp of fur underneath his nostrils to check that breathing has stopped
- Open his mouth, pull the tongue forward, and make sure there are no obstructions. Be careful that the dog does not bite you, when putting your fingers in his mouth.
- If he does not start breathing, extend his head so that the nose is pointing forwards. Clamp the mouth down and blow into the nose around 20 times every 60 seconds. If his heart doesn't start beating, push on his chest just behind the front legs once a second. For every 15 compressions, breathe twice into the nose. After doing this for three minutes and he still hasn't recovered, it is unlikely that he will.

CHAPTER 14

Cairn Terrier Legal Requirements: What is Needed?

E very country has their own set of legal requirements for owning a dog. Before buying a Cairn Terrier, it is important to check with your local authority concerning the laws you will need to be in compliance with.

Vaccines: As soon as you have purchased your Cairn Terrier, take him to the vet. It is even better if you can do so before bringing him home. Regardless of the country you are in, it is advised that you bring the vaccination records from the owner or breeder, and if you can, provide the name of the vet who originally treated and vaccinated the litter. There are two categories of vaccines in every country:

1. Core vaccines: They are essential for your Cairn Terrier
2. Non-core vaccines: They are not essential for your Cairn Terrier

Dog Licensing: Depending on the country (and the city or state in the country, in some cases) in which you live, there is a possibility that you will need to license your Cairn Terrier, once you have purchased him. It is important to find out this information before bringing your dog home, to avoid being in violation of the law.

Mandatory Vaccinations For Your Cairn Terrier In The United States

According to the American Animal Hospital Association (AAHA) vaccine guidelines, the following vaccines are mandatory for all Cairn Terriers in America:

- Canine parvovirus
- Canine adenovirus-2 (hepatitis)
- Canine distemper virus
- Rabies Virus

Non-Core Vaccines

- Leptospirosis
- Lyme Disease
- Kennel Cough

Licensing Requirements For Owning a Cairn Terrier In The United States

The majority of states require Cairn Terrier owners to license their pets. It is important to check the licensing requirements with your city or county as soon as you get your dog. Any Cairn Terrier owner found without a license, is liable for a fine.

Mandatory Vaccinations For Your Cairn Terrier In The UK

According to The World Small Animal Veterinary Association, the core vaccines recommended for all dogs in the United Kingdom are as follows:

- Canine Distemper
- Canine Parvovirus
- Canine Hepatitis
- Adenovirus

Non-core vaccines include the following:

- Canine Parainfluenza Virus (Kennel Cough)
- Canine Herpes Virus
- Rabies

Licensing Requirements For Owning a Cairn Terrier In The UK

You do not need a license to own a dog in the United Kingdom. These requirements were abolished in 1987.

Mandatory Vaccinations For Your Cairn Terrier In Canada

According to The Canadian Veterinary Medical Association the core vaccines recommended for all dogs in Canada are as follows:

- Canine Distemper
- Infectious Canine Hepatitis

- Canine Parvovirus
- Rabies

Non-core vaccines include the following:

- Bordetellosis
- Canine Parainfluenza Virus
- Leptospirosis
- Borreliosis (Lyme diseases)
- Coronavirus

Licensing Requirements For Owning a Cairn Terrier In Canada

Every territory in Canada requires that your dog is licensed. However, it is important that you check the requirements within your city or town because each location has got a different set of regulations. Any Cairn Terrier owner found without a license is liable for a fine.

CHAPTER 15

Conclusion to the Cairn Terrier

So, you have arrived at the end of the book! Congratulations, some of you have either decided that a Cairn Terrier is not for you, some of you may have already purchased one, some of you might be on your way to make a purchase, or you may be well into your journey. Either way, I hope I have provided you with enough information to succeed and thrive with your Cairn Terrier, if you have decided this is the breed for you.

Remember, regardless of the breed, dogs are precious animals, they are a gift to mankind, and they should be treated as such. Dogs are for life, if you are not ready to make a lifelong commitment, you might want to reconsider. But before you make your final decision, here are some important points to think about:

• Are you willing to spend as long as it takes to train your Cairn Terrier? All dogs are different, just because it took your brother's puppy two hours to learn the sit command, doesn't mean you should expect the same results. You will need a lot of patience to ensure that your dog is well trained.

- How much time do you have to devote to playing with your dog each day? Cairn Terriers need between 1-2 hours of playtime every day. Consistent playtime and exercise will ensure that your dog is well-behaved and well trained.

- You will need to take your dog out first thing in the morning. Owning a dog is like having a child, he comes first. You will have to abolish your normal routine of having a cup of coffee and reading a newspaper as soon as you wake up. Your dog's needs come first.

- Your Cairn Terrier will need to interact with other dogs and people to ensure that he is well-rounded and capable of socializing outside of the environment he is used to.

- Who will finance your dog's needs? Vet bills, food, toys, and accessories, dogs cost money. You will need to set a budget to ensure that you can afford to keep a dog for the long term.

- You must spend time with your dog. Spending time with your Cairn Terrier does not stop at taking your dog for walks and training. Watching TV together, going shopping, taking him to events are all important. Dogs are social creatures; their pack is now you and your family, and they will rely on you for social interaction.

Well, that's about it for now, but before you go, there's one more chapter I'd like you to have a look at.........

Bonus Chapter: Your Trusted Cairn Terrier Resource List

I n this final chapter, you will find some additional information to further assist you with your Cairn Terrier.

Buying a Cairn Terrier will be the best decision you have ever made.

Cairn Terrier Association – Will I Need To Join a Cairn Terrier Association?

It is not mandatory that you join a Cairn Terrier club or association, but you can if you wish. Below is a list of clubs in your country.

United States: http://cairnterrier.org/
United Kingdom: http://www.thecairnterrierclub.co.uk/
Canada: http://www.cairnterrierclub.ca/
Australia: https://www.cairnsnsw.com/

Cairn Terrier Westminster Dog Show – What Do I Need To Know About The Event?

The Westminster dog show is an annual event held on the second Monday and Tuesday of February. The exhibition takes place in New York city at Madison Square Garden, and has been dubbed the Olympics of dog shows.

Westminster is a conformation show; each dog is judged according to standards penned by the members of every parent breed club. This standard defines the ideal temperament, movement and structure of each breed, as well as information such as coat color, eye and ear placement, and tail. The main aim of conformation dog shows is to judge breeding stock; therefore, dogs entered into the show cannot be neutered or spayed, they must be intact. Before a dog can enter Westminster, they must have participated in several other shows throughout the country.

Puppies can attend classes to become Westminster show ready, from the age of six months. Male and females are trained separately, after approximately six classes, the winner from each class is judged again for the best male or female in each breed. They are awarded points according to the number of dogs from their breed that were entered into the competition. If enough dogs from the breed entered, the show is considered a major. Once a dog has accumulated 15 points, and wins two major shows, he becomes a champion.

In 2013, the rules were changed, allowing dogs who have accumulated one major win but not yet completed their championship to enter Westminster. In 2014, the Masters Agility Championship was added to the competition. It is held on the Saturday prior to conformation breed judging. It is open to mixed-breed dogs competing at the Excellent or Masters level of the sport; there are 225 entries available. To qualify, entrants must pass two agility courses with weave poles, tunnels, jumps and more.

Cairn Terrier Rescue Organizations – What Happens To a Mistreated Cairn Terrier Dog?

If you witness a Cairn Terrier or any other animal being mistreated, call the police. It is important that you keep yourself safe, so it is not advised that you go and intervene, you will be of no help to anyone if you are injured. Also, you might scare the perpetrator, and cause them to run away with the dog. If this happens, the police may not be able to trace the person, preventing the dog from getting the help that it needs.

Finally, it is important to remember that dogs are extremely loyal, even if they are being abused and they see someone getting involved in an argument with their owner, they could attack you.

Therefore, the best thing to do is call the police and do what they ask until they arrive.

You can also report the abuse to an animal rescue center:

United Kingdom: RSPCA: https://www.rspca.org.uk
Canada: SPCA: https://spca.bc.ca/
United States: ASPCA: https://www.aspca.org/
Australia: RSPCA: https://www.rspca.org.au

Cairn Terrier Breeders USA – Where Can I Find Cairn Terrier Breeders In The USA?

https://www.thekennelclub.org.uk/services/public/acbr/Default.aspx?breed=Cairn+Terrier

http://cairnterrier.org/index.php/Breeders/list-by-state

https://www.yellowbrickrdkennels.com/about-us

http://www.bodockridgekennel.com/home/

http://pebblerockcairns.com/index1.htm

Cairn Terrier Puppies For Sale USA - Where Can I Buy Cairn Terrier Puppies In The USA

https://marketplace.akc.org/puppies/cairn-terrier

https://www.adoptapet.com/s/adopt-a-cairn-terrier

https://www.marmascairnterriers.com/

https://puppyfinder.com/cairn-terrier-puppies-for-sale

https://www.nextdaypets.com/Cairn-Terrier.htm

Cairn Terrier Breeders Australia – Where Can I Find Cairn Terrier Breeders In Australia?

https://www.dogzonline.com.au/breeds/breeders/cairn-terrier.asp

https://perfectpets.com.au/pets/dogs/dog-breeds/dog-breeders/cairn-terrier

https://www.dogs4sale.com.au/Breeds/Cairn_Terrier/Breeders.htm

http://www.joymont.com/

http://www.lochrincairn.com/

Cairn Terrier Puppies For Sale Australia – Where Can I Buy Cairn Terrier Puppies In Australia?

https://www.cubberoo.com/default.asp

https://www.animalinfo.com.au/

Cairn Terrier Breeders UK – Where Can I Find Cairn Terrier Breeders In The UK?

https://carradinecairns.co.uk/

http://www.cairn-terriers.co.uk/

http://www.tycadno.freeuk.com/puppy.html

https://www.lindcolydogs.co.uk/

Cairn Terrier Puppies For Sale UK - Where Can I Buy Cairn Terrier Puppies In The UK?

https://www.pets4homes.co.uk/sale/dogs/cairn-terrier/

http://www.thecairnterrierclub.co.uk/

https://www.thekennelclub.org.uk/

Cairn Terrier Breeders In Canada – Where Can I Find Cairn Terrier Breeders In Canada?

http://www.cairnterrierclub.ca/breeders.html

https://www.pawsitivepuppies.com/meet-jan/

http://www.magisterialkennels.com/terriers.html

http://www.cairn-terrier.ca/cairn-en/cairn-home.html

https://www.gatewaycairns.com/

Cairn Terrier Puppies For Sale In Canada – Where Can I Buy Cairn Terrier Puppies In Canada?

http://www.cairn-terrier.ca/cairn-en/cairn-puppies.html

https://canadiandogs.com/cairn-terrier-puppies-canada/

http://www.nicepetsincanada.com/ontario/pets/cairn+terrier/

https://www.doggies.com/Cairn_Terrier/Ontario

Made in the USA
Las Vegas, NV
16 November 2021